forget THE former

A Glimpse Into Redemptive Reality

Leigh Allison

Paperback: 978-1-964035-37-6
eBook: 978-1-964035-38-3
Library of Congress Control Number: 2024918910

This is a work of nonfiction.

SWEETSPIRE LITERATURE
——— MANAGEMENT ———

TABLE OF CONTENTS

DEDICATION

To my dear friend, Jenny Hogan.

Somehow, through inspiring conversation, challenge, laughter and tears, you have been God's choice to drive me to do more than I have believed possible.

Thank you for being my true friend.

ACKNOWLEDGEMENTS

Erica Jade is the first person who comes to mind in those I wish to thank for this reprint edition. I honestly believe that Erica is the only one who could have engineered me through these months to complete the work.

There exists in our world an enormous fear and doubt about engaging in business unless there is a personal connection. Add to this, the international dimension. Friends, family, and financial institutions panic.

However, from the beginning, my intuition registered that I trust Erica. I am really delighted to have someone so experienced and capable to work with. Further, it is not simply Erica's skills I value, it is her indescribable gift of being 'herself'.

Other people I wish to thank for being with me on this journey of life are:

Ann Godwin, Annie Short, Belinda Addison, Caroline Lattin, Dr Liza Siebuhr, Dr Rodney T Hall, Jan Keogh, Janet Lieu Sorbo, Judith & Gary Stewart, Kim Kelly, Louisa Francini, Mary Wong, Maureen McComb, Mildred Rihia, Penelope Lawson, Regina Manz, Stephanie Collins, Yanetta Serbasio.

Each name has stories untold, and not enough space to give them the highlights they deserve. Such happy memories! The making of more fabulous times together, are ready to plan for. Imagine that!

PREFACE

Leigh and I have been close friends for twenty years. She has written *Forget the Former* with the heartbeat of where she's been. Her quest for peace has been an amazing journey, and the awesome power of God has brought her to victory. Over the years I have seen many changes in Leigh. When I first met her, I wondered what was happening. Leigh has a wealth of professional experience in the helping field. Then Bang! Thoughts of despair and insecurities would flood back. Often I watched helplessly. The depression was severe and seemed to come when people spoke or reacted negatively to Leigh, implying "you'll always be like this." I could see the pain. This had become a vicious cycle where sickness would come because it was expected to come: a self-fulfilling prophecy. Each specialist seemed to know best. One of the things this book typifies is what goes on in people's minds when they are given a label. Words can pierce the soul. Yet Jesus rescued her.

Leigh had never wanted to "just survive." She wanted to live. Not only did Leigh make it through these difficult in-between years, she came to know that God would use her gifts and experience to a greater degree. "Line upon line, precept upon precept," her faith grew. This has encouraged me. I thought I was living until I saw, in her life, there was so much more through faith in God.

We see people's lives in landmarks. During our friendship, Leigh's first landmark was when she purchased her first home. This was a sign of survival after the severe breakdown that tagged her as being schizophrenic. Another tag, bipolar disorder, was given later. The next landmark was when Leigh rededicated her life to the Lord. From mere survival, she began to see the steps to recovery. Then followed the tape series, *Col Stringer Teaches on the Mind*. It gave her a handle on how to apply the Word of God in her life. For hours a day and through the night, Leigh would listen to tapes of God's Word: to know who she is in Christ. It was not what the world or people said about her that mattered. It was who God says she is. Repeating Scriptures like, "I can do all things through Christ who strengthens me," would be said in batches of one hundred at a time. Then Scripture after Scripture followed. It wasn't rote. It was food to her mind that made her able to "run and not grow weary."

Rhema Bible Training Centre, Gold Coast, was a landmark too, and Leigh graduated to a purposeful life. As God's child, she now expected abundance. The Lord Jesus Christ surely has been her Advocate in the heavenly realm. As Leigh became stronger in the knowledge of Jesus Christ, the Spirit of God strengthened the Word from her head to her heart, so that her trust in the Lord is absolute. Leigh knows there is no one else we can trust.

Most recently, of course, is the landmark of writing this book. In *Forget the Former*, Leigh shows we don't have to keep slipping and going back to be redeemed. Once forgiven, we cannot be retried. Anyone can have this assurance, if they choose God's way. I owe my walk with the Lord, partly to Leigh, because she is steadfast. She didn't pacify me or tickle my ears. She simply said, "There is a way: a way that is lasting. Not just a fad! If you want your life to have meaning, the only way is through the Lord Jesus Christ." Leigh's life is an example of God's redeeming love.

There are many people who are at the place of, "Help! I want to get out of where I am." Many need this book, as it portrays the escape from Darkness to Light: the hope that is realized. *Forget the Former* is another lifeline to connect us to the Advocate we have with our heavenly Father.

Jenny Hogan Director
Victory Mountain Ministries MS 366, Rosewood
QLD 4340
Australia

INTRODUCTION

The point of when a person realizes that "enough is enough" is a significant experience. If a person does not know his or her rights, that person has none. This includes their spiritual rights. Neglect of the spiritual realm is like looking at the ceiling and being ignorant of the sky. Tides obey the laws of creation, and balance in the midst of storms is found only in the One who created all things. There is a limit to the degree that anyone can effect change themselves. Self-help books alone cannot satisfy.

Anyone who has suffered a devastating event, chronic illness, long-term problem, or grief is likely to be in an inner debate with God. In this book, I relate experiences that are mine to a degree, but I also describe them in general terms, so that I can be a point of identification for others who are experiencing emotional and mental trauma. Having been so low as to wonder if it was worth the effort to try to get up again, I doubted whether there could even be a God.

Yet a curious thing happened. Although I did not want to recover, I began to recover. The pleasantness of sunshine and the beauty of the sky and flowers were absorbed by my senses and into my soul. Snippets of my early Christian upbringing became thoughts that seemed to think toward God for me. I have a God who looked for me first, took the death penalty that was my due, and gave me everything of value.

Through a mixture of emotions, we want God to explain our suffering. However, most people have lived much of their lives before ever asking the pertinent questions. For the non-Christian, this question is, "What do I believe about Jesus Christ, and am I informed?" For the Christian, the question is, "What does redemption mean to me, and am I living it?"

In redemption through Jesus Christ, a person becomes one with Him, and thus receives his very true nature. The Christian life involves becoming who one already is in Christ. "Appropriation" is very simply, "making it mine." When a person knows that they have been redeemed, that redemption has to then be put into practice: "I am forgiven. I forgive those who have hurt me. The past is gone. I let the past go. God does not condemn me. I do not condemn myself. I renew my mind to what God says and obey His Word. I affirm my identity in Christ."

There is enormous evidence of the healing and restoring power through Jesus Christ to whom I owe my own restoration. Without a relationship with Him, I could not have sustained the will to live through the dark times.

This book is strongly based on Scripture. I encourage you to relate the story to the actual Scripture passages. They are set out in detail for three purposes: to provide evidence of a sound biblical framework; to be used for specific needs, such as forgiveness; and for meditation.

The depiction of the loveliness of Jesus Christ as my Advocate shows why He should be desired by all people. He is the Man of light who divided time, separated truth from deception, exchanged sorrow for joy, and kept my past in the past, in order to give me a future. As the Advocate, He quiets the turmoil of war in every person's heart, who permits it, and restores their peace.

I hope you, the dear reader, will begin to make the choices that will give you the keys to ultimately bring you the answers you desire.

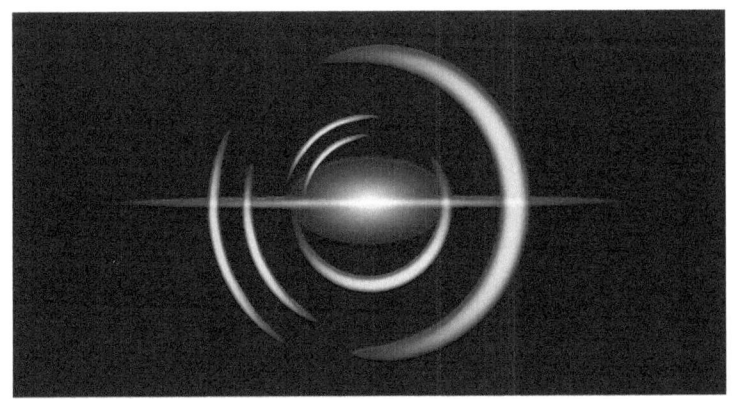

A GLIMPSE OF GLORY, MAJESTY AND MIGHT

Mysterious Wheels

More than 2500 years ago, these words were written…

An ancient man saw the heavens open, and he glimpsed the glory of the upper world. Then his soul knew its destitution. All of him was seen and known. The consequences held him in dread, especially of judgment.

A mystery of the spirit, like a wheel within a wheel, was unfolding.

A whirlwind created a great cloud with flaming fire, engulfing itself in its brilliance, as it descended from the north. Clarity came by the wind, and then there was stillness. He was terrified, yet aware that this was preparation for understanding.

Four angelic beings emerged: They were similar to men. As he looked more closely, he saw that the beings each had four faces and four wings with hands under their wings. They stood firm and steady, united and ready for action. Emerging from the fiery cloud, they radiated the color of burnished brass. Their wings were joined to one another for straightness of purpose: to go to the four corners of the world.

The man knew he was seeing in symbols. The faces of the beings were of a man, a lion, an ox and an eagle, to signify intelligence and reason, strength and courage, diligence and patience and the ability to see into divine mysteries.

As the beings stretched toward heaven, he discerned the attributes of piety and devotion, faith and hope, and tenderness and sincerity of heart.

Suddenly one wheel appeared on the earth, closely connected to the beings. The wheel was the color of the sea. Then the wheel became four wheels, as it were, wheels within a wheel, encompassing every direction and being present in every place.

In awe the man thought: "I cannot comprehend such riches of wisdom and knowledge." With renewed dread, he saw that the rims of the wheels were full of eyes. No one can hide. All is seen.

Each time the creatures were elevated from the earth and its ways, the wheels lifted up. Ascending, a translucent sphere separated earth from the place of glory, for the upper world is that which inspects and influences the events of earth. Then a huge noise made by the wings of the creatures urgently directed the man to a sound as of the voice of the Almighty, like the noise of an army.

Even in this visionary state, by the eye of faith, he witnessed the magnificence and splendor of the appearance of a throne as clear as sapphire. Upon it sat the figure of a Man clothed with brilliant light. A rainbow appeared to signify majesty and mercy.

He fell upon his face, for this is glory.

(A paraphrase of Ezekiel 1:4-28)

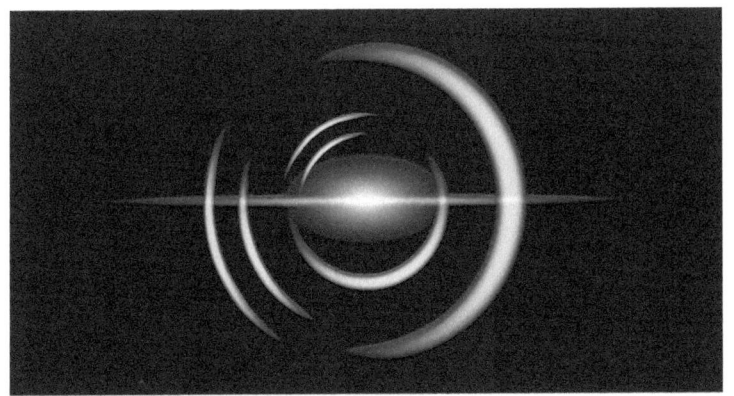

Chapter One

IN THE MIDST OF TURMOIL

The First Wheel

Possibilities soared as, in her mind's eye, the woman was part of a parade with brass bands and streamers and shouts of celebration. Draped in rich, royal purple, she rode in the open-topped limousine, exhilarating in the moment.

Victory was the reward for overcoming struggle. She knew that "no one arrives," yet some progressed more than others. Life's journey went from one bend in the road to the next, but no individual could totally determine their own fate. A multitude of external forces, even supernatural power, reduced self-power to a mere fraction.

The woman's path of discovery had begun with a few simple words on a page: "Now choose life." She was momentarily surprised because it was so obvious. A price for change had to be paid, and that price was to leave the past behind. Consequently, a bridge formed between hopelessness and fulfilment. Her thoughts developed into those of beauty and loveliness, substituting for those of many years making when she pretended not to notice life. She was now certain that there was profit in adversity. This was her season to be blessed. Darkness rolled back. Light had come.

As far as she knew, the journey began yesterday, although this period of time seemed too small to account for its significance. It was only a day ago when she was sitting in a quiet courtyard, motionless except for her concentrating eyes. A series of art gallery images registered in her consciousness. With the click of an imaginary camera, a picture of her emerged: pleasantly dressed, apparently composed and well-suited to blend into any faceless crowd. The woman's straight posture had the look of a survivor who had overcome many problems in her life. Yet the struggle wasn't over. She thought, *I've always had everything I needed. Why don't I want to live?*

Looking down, the woman saw only a small circle of paved ground. However, when she looked up, she could see the sky in an arc from horizon to horizon. The clouds were being reshaped with wisps and puffs. Would they build to rain-filled swells later? Gazing upward lifted her spirits. The colors of the sky could lick the edge of a cloud with a hint, or blast the whole surface in rich, dense, shining, pure yellows and reds.

If only I could enjoy this beauty without feeling that life was pointless, she thought. *The sky is spectacular, even when it's cloudless blue. It's free—as free for me as for anyone else. I really want to receive this pleasure. I will decide to hold and enjoy it as a gift to me. I see myself holding an armful of pleasure, ethereal though it is. I'm going to look at the sky and see the broader picture, instead of the dry patch of ground around my feet.*

Another image slid across the first one, filtered through light gray. Like a spectator, the woman could see her workplace and the faces of her co-workers. They would probably have described her as inexpressive, yet they did not understand her actual state. Any brief exchange with them was filled with multiple questions. Instead of noticing anything positive, like a kind expression or gentle voice, she scanned every face for telltale signs of rejection. *Where does this turmoil come from?* she wondered. She would discover that the true answer to a question is not always the literal one.

The next image that passed through her mind was that of an amusement arcade mirror. It distorted and magnified her image, as if all her faults were clearly visible. The woman realized that she had formed a habit of ignoring pleasant thoughts. Pressure had been building in her mind, brought on by vivid memories of disappointment.

The grainy dimness of the next picture took her aback. It was a blurred image of herself, as if one picture had been superimposed on another, like a box within a box. Her interior world had become more real than the physical world about her.

All my childhood dreams are simply wishful thinking, not likely to come true, she thought. In this downward mental spiral, her soul was filled with a sense of having lost something she never possessed. She had a distance to go to have peace within, and to have the confidence to be who she was made to be.

The books the woman had read helped somewhat: "Fix your thoughts and you fix your feelings," they admonished. Yet a threatening image of her metamorphosing into a mythic beast was the next image to hit her awareness. What she needed was cohesion. Somehow her outward control, inward volatility and eerie sense of a fire gone out had to be replaced by wholeness. There must be a way to assimilate her distress so that she did not breathe the hot ash and embers of pent-up emotion upon unsuspecting people.

The word "tactics" was written like skywriting after that image. She knew in agonizing frustration how stupid it was to be negative, although a vague hope encouraged her—choose to expect her life to be blessed and she may no longer be afflicted. A little relief came. Optimistic people were, almost without exception, happy and successful. *Why don't I just choose this way of life? Surely, it would be just as easy to say, "I can," instead of "I can't," and "I care," instead of "Who cares?"* The woman was sure that pleasure and success were closely related. They both seemed to be found in people who were satisfied with their existence. Success meant achievement. Her habit had been to evaluate a particular experience by the feelings that emerged from it. She had sadly found that achievement could be empty. Feelings exasperated her. They didn't listen to reason, they went off on tangents, and they made a big thing of trivialities. She craved emotional balance.

The picture show continued. The woman's mind portrayed her with heavy weights from a gymnasium strapped to her body. She questioned who she should be, and how she should be. Previously she had deduced that failure must have been caused by her own malfunction. *Is that what happened to me? Have I been the one to give myself the expectations, not others? Have I been the one to call an experience a "failure," despite the facts, simply because my feelings were uncomfortable?*

A sad image that seeped into the woman's heart showed her that her soul had been torn in several ways: through expectations within and without; through her own thoughts and feelings; through rules and conscience. In her view, conscience was higher than the rules. It was time to put one of her important, yet pleasureless achievements on the imaginary scales of objectivity.

This day I call heaven and earth as witnesses against you that I have set before you life and death, blessings and curses. Now choose life, so that you and your children may live (Deuteronomy 30:10).

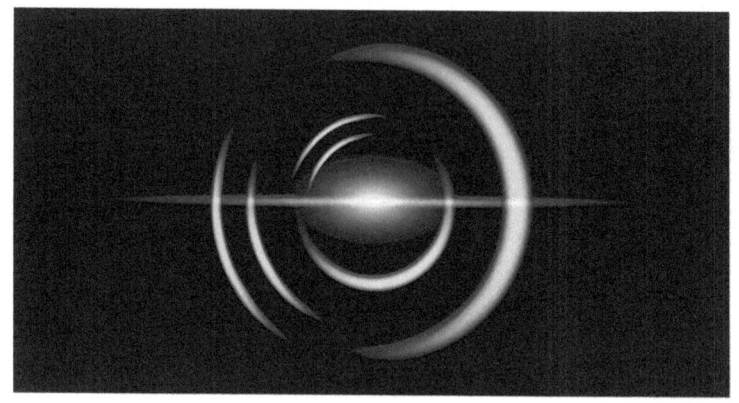

Chapter Two

A SHAFT OF POSSIBILITY

The Second Wheel

H ers had not been the only soul divided. Affectionately, the woman visualized a 14-year-old boy who had drawn the chasm of his parents' divorce into his being. How he was rescued from the continued splitting of his mind was wonderfully simple. For several months, she had contact with him repeatedly, supporting him in his agony. He often directed his inner turmoil outward, in abuse to whomever was near. The woman recognized his pattern.

One day years before, the woman's anger had caused her to drop her caring shield, and she instinctively struck back against the boy with her words. He temporarily broke like a fallen mirror, with protracted loud cries of emotional pain, defensive hostility and tears. Despite his provocation, he had not suffered careless, unreasonable retaliation before from her. Suddenly he lay face down, exhausted. He was unable to speak for hours. She had a choice: to be the adult who was always right when it came to juveniles, or to admit her awful misjudgment and humbly ask for his forgiveness. She chose the latter, expecting vengeance. Yet as he let go of this in favor of peace, she saw the awesome force of giving dignity through an apology. Remarkably, after a short conversation, he was able to accept his parents' divorce. Someone had said the word "sorry"—he was not at fault.

The boy had faced the woman as she wrestled with the choice of accepting or evading responsibility. With detachment, she weighed her achievements separately from her feelings, and faced another choice: to dwell on the mistake or to enjoy the ending. Credit was due for her self-effacing request for forgiveness. Without that, there would have been continual chafing to the devastating wound concerning the divorce. With her intense remorse, she had touched his heart in the place where trust resides, and it was like ointment to his soul. The sides of his wound closed together cleanly.

Years separated the transforming experience for the boy and this day of images. However, her mind had attended only to the pain she'd brought the boy. Suddenly she thought, I *am amazed at the result. It worked out for the best. Now I can see that it's my mixture of emotions that robs me of the thrill of his breakthrough. My negativity, though, isn't just a connecting thread* in my life—it's a fibrous rope tied around my mind. It's easier for me to remember my failures than any success. I want to change. I must change.

Two images of her, as photographs in separate frames appeared, as if a conversation were taking place. The woman realized, "No risk, no gain." Through a series of inner debates, she began to convince herself to allow change to proceed. A shaft of possibility, like faint sunshine, touched her. *Perhaps another person can help me to discover qualities that are good, likeable and light inside me. Despite everything, I sense these do exist.* The woman intensely believed that every life had value, and even though her own life felt shriveled, it must have value, too. *I need to express who I really am—when I know. If I just vent my emotions, my words will almost certainly wound, as the boy found out.*

Making connections between these pictures, the woman imagined her emotions as phantoms that visited her from another existence. They were simply something that happened. Despair was heavy and flat; disappointment was grim and tight-lipped; sorrow was a wet face; meaninglessness and hopelessness were twins who mocked her desire to live. She wondered whether she would continue to fight to survive if she broke out of this circle of unpleasant emotions, or whether she would simply become a shell filled with lethargy. Could she take this risk? At least she knew what to expect of life, even though she was uncomfortable. Change frightened her because there were no guarantees. So it was, excuses argued with her: *Will it be worth rocking the boat? Yet I must take responsibility for my life. I desperately want to have something good to show for having existed: to stand for something worthwhile. I want to be satisfied that I'm doing my best. There will always be those who will ridicule me for trying to be useful.*

The woman hoped that life would get better. The images moved on. The woman saw herself in a ship's lifebelt. She had one thing to cling to: her capacity to reason. *I have to face my self-justification that seeks any way to blame others. These are my feelings! My words! My actions! I can't blame anyone else! I must find a way to think and react differently.* The woman knew it was imperative for her to build an image of herself that she could accept—a new, strong identity that would take her outside the droning circle of her own thoughts.

For there is nothing hidden that will not be disclosed, and nothing concealed that will not be known or brought out into the open (Luke 8:17).

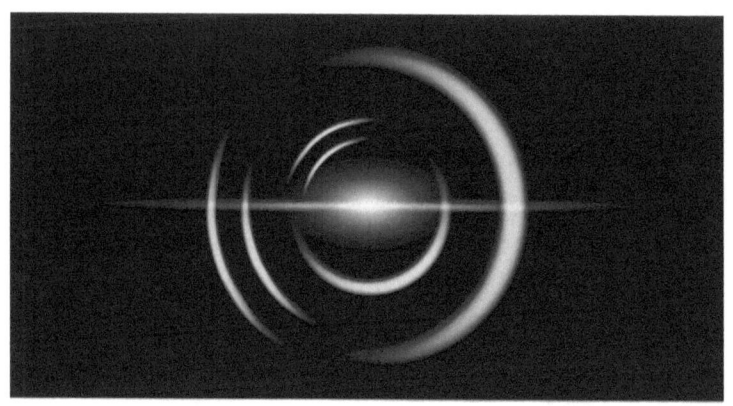

Chapter Three

UNDOING HABIT-TRAPS

The Third Wheel

I need passion and perseverance to push through these habit-traps. If I could only know for sure whether God is real or not .... Her thoughts trailed off. It was paradoxical to ask, "Is there a God?" for it already implied a concept of God who is a person and not just a force.

She thought of the image of her gazing at a rainbow in the sky. *Rainbows contain a promise, don't they?* People professed not to believe in "God," yet they nevertheless referred to Him in everyday speech. Therefore, in this way He existed for them. Even if she spoke only to the air, this woman decided to ask and to keep on asking questions, compelled to find the answers she so desperately needed.

Devoid of peace and rest, she paused for a moment to think of the 14-year-old boy. It was curious how a mistake could be the catalyst for remarkable change. Then she realized that it wasn't the mistake that sparked the change—it was the response. A mistake was a mistake, but it was like a random factor that could change the whole process of events. Good could come out of bad. Her focus on her mistakes was really a waste of mental and emotional energy that did not allow her to move forward. Not every mistake could be corrected. That was a fact that affected everyone. However, consequences were available for conversion.

The woman thought, *If I'm to think, act and feel differently, my old habits will have to go. No matter how difficult this will be, I must make the effort.* Her hope felt strengthened, like a muscle that had been exercised, bringing a hint of a smile to her face. For the first time in many years, she believed that her life would improve. Not only did her problems with anger and despair distress her, but others also. With a healthy curiosity, she wondered, *What will the new "me" be like?*

Obviously, the future only existed in her imagination. There she was: a little child who lived in her dreams. Sadly, years of dreary, daily existence had squashed them. The woman resolved to imagine who she wanted to be, and not to get caught in a bog of accepting a future that others in her past expected. Their expectations would inevitably be of a poorer kind. No!

She couldn't restrict herself in that way. Spontaneously, she looked at the sky again, and it seemed to open up, as a window through which she could see vast galaxies and then blank space. Meaning was not found in just this little planet of earth, for everything was part of a whole that had no end. Without meaning, how could she live? Living with the knowledge of constant futility would be the path to destruction. She decided that the magnificence of creation surely held the key.

I'm going to go into a rehearsal for a happy and successful life. The new image is going to be so real to me that I will act it into existence. Instant-replay days of my failures are over. I've been like so many people who are living cautious, trapped lives. All that brings is frustrated dreams. Change is there! Change is ready and waiting! My desire is the catalyst. I am putting the key in the ignition, and this engine will go forward with great power. This tiny spark will lead to a great light.

Ask and it will be given to you; seek and you will find; knock and the door will be opened to you. For everyone who asks receives; he who seeks finds; and to him who knocks, the door will be opened (Matthew 7:7-8).

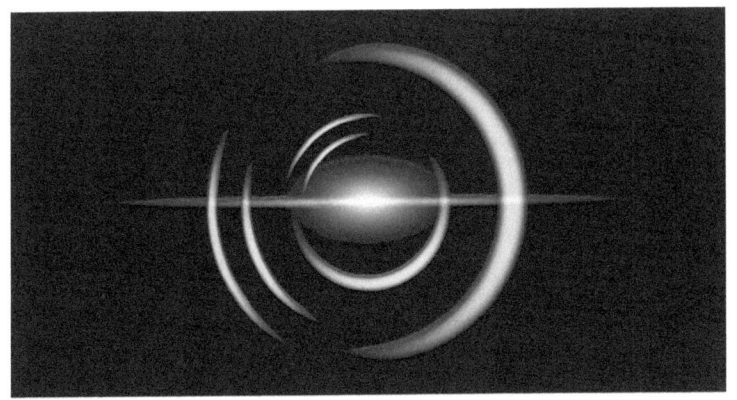

Chapter Four

SURGING TERROR AND PURE TRUST

The Fourth Wheel

The engine certainly kicked into gear, although not the way the woman expected. It was as if a camera were rolling and a director had called, "Action!" Instantly, as if in a dream, she stood before the courtroom of heaven. In the ethereal atmosphere, her body felt light. The air was clean to inhale, although her surroundings were not the majestic grandeur she expected heaven to be. Somewhat bewildered, she decided that she must be in heaven because she was not on earth, and certainly she was not in the hell described in books.

There was before her a long bench of good quality wood, two shorter side-benches and a few rows of straight-backed, yet comfortable chairs. What she saw seemed hazy; it was as if the perimeter of the room faded out. Strangely, she felt neither afraid nor exhilarated, although she realized that she had stepped aside from ordinary life. It was like participating in a movie without a script.

Into her line of sight came three men—two of them in focus and one indistinct. The first man was dressed elegantly and stylishly, the second one extravagantly. Then a fleeting metamorphosis occurred in the second figure, revealing grotesque features upon which she could barely keep her gaze. The woman felt troubled and sickened. It was as if she could see his motives, and they were lethal. His trademark was glaring arrogance. Her ears rang with a silent scream of terror, her hands were clammy, and her heart was racing.

What is real? The second man terrifies me. I'm frozen to this spot by his staring hate. Body, pull me away from this predator, this evil. He wants to capture me, to make me his victim—a trophy in a hideous contest. God! If You are there, look my way! My whole body is churning. I'm fighting to escape from being swallowed into a black void.

From that moment, she called this being Darkness. Just as quickly as it appeared, his grotesque image receded into his former extravagant image. She gathered her thoughts that seemed to have been sent flying like papers in the wind. Surely that creature was the result of taking free will to the extreme. *He does what he wants, when he wants and how he wants, without regard to anyone else. No! Not quite! He just thinks he can. Megalomaniacs do that,* she realized.

There was a pause.

The woman's gaze turned toward the first individual in the courtroom. His robe was cut of the finest cloth, yet it was simple in design. Something captivated her about his face. His expression was clear, open and trustworthy. Thinking about it, she decided that innocence with knowledge was a rare combination. Again she experienced the ability to look into his heart, as she had done with Darkness. What a difference his attitude was! So pure! *Why don't I repulse him? I know all of my wrongs,* she thought. Guilt tried to prevent her from standing in the same room as this man of virtue. Huge sorrow surfaced from a cavern in her mind as she stood in the man's presence. However, it wasn't the murky type of sorrow to which she was accustomed. It acted to clean her thoughts as tears of remorse painfully swelled and drained from her eyes. She held back her weeping until it could be restrained no longer. It hurt! Her chest and throat wanted to block the pain. The noise of her crying in lonely despair embarrassed her. Until this point in her life, she had maintained an image of competence through her self-control. *I'm exposed. What else will be uncovered? Yet this man is different. He seems to infuse me with warmth and dispel my fears.*

A momentary touch of expectancy, like a puff of breeze, refreshed her. The woman called this one Lightman and loved him instantly. She was captivated. His presence was pleasant, almost fragrant, and he had a voice that carried an echo like the sound of the sea in a shell. In his eyes she saw timeless kindness. Essentially, he was strong, although she could see that he preferred to cover it as if with a soft glove.

The third figure in the Courtroom gave her the impression of a judge. She evaded his gaze, shuddering with the foreboding that he could unleash punishment upon her. By not looking at him, it was as if he was not there and so could not convict her. At the same time, she knew that this strategy would not be effective.

This was a spiritual zone, as real as the physical ones of touch, taste, sight, hearing and smell she experienced on earth. It was no stretch for her to consider people as spirit-beings. However, in this peculiar state, her whole body suddenly felt heavy, and she sensed that she was facing accumulated powers. How could she possibly fend off wicked spirit beings? Fear swept over her, like the awareness of being stalked. The experience of this place was inexplicable.

Yes! I'm awake in this examination—the examination of my soul. This is astonishing! How can it be that this is happening to me? Am I going mad? Flesh-and-blood people can at least be seen.

However, the strongest presence, Light-man, was that of a grand ally.

Who is the liar? It is the man who denies that Jesus is the Christ. Such a man is the antichrist—he denies the Father and the Son (1 John 2:22).

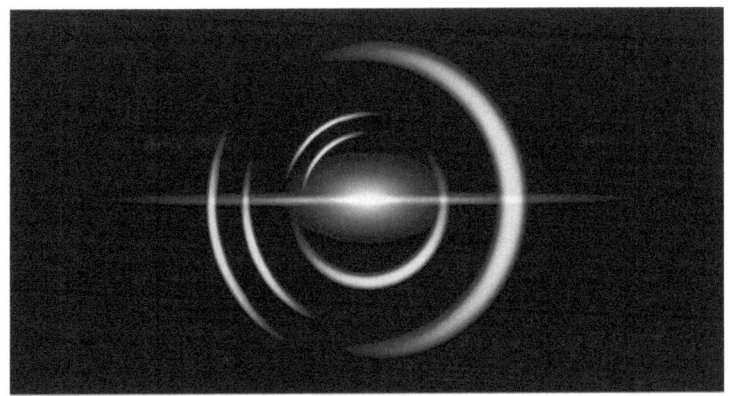

Chapter Five

TORN FABRIC OF LIFE

The Fifth Wheel

With the emergence of the figures in this court, she perceived two worlds in conflict: one dark, one light. In the world from which she had come, laws were needed as the external means to subdue behavior that worked against peace. But knowing what was right and doing it were two different things. Everyone knew that punishment for murder was common sense. If killing was tolerated, anyone could be killed. Yet she saw the potential for everyone to be violent.

The human heart had its own dark imprint. Her emotions, at times erupting into words and behavior, told her this, as they spilled their molten heat and choking ash onto innocent people.

The law's an afterthought: It's too late. It's so clear that voluntary peace makes more sense, not prison and punishment. If only humanity concentrated on the do's instead of the do-not's. Love one another! Do good to those who hate you! Turn the other cheek! It's absurd that most of us still don't learn.

The woman wanted to shake people, and herself, and say: "Wake up! Don't think you can be logical about the dark side of human nature! Being more rational and scientific won't make the world run peacefully. Corrupt people in powerful positions inflict the most inhumane abuses, and these are the products of their minds. It's so obvious! No human being can possibly be the pattern for morality."

She seized these insights that might make her life's path more negotiable. Pictured in her mind was society, as part of an engineer's plan, with reason and science being the steel spans of a bridge. She saw the futility of trying to build such a structure over the Pacific Ocean. Humanity thought that it could address life's problems with theories, yet these were only disjointed fragments. Sure, knowledge had its place. However, here in the courtroom of heaven, she was forming a new, wonderful, exciting and exhilarating perspective.

The courtroom's exceptional atmosphere drew her further into the examination of her life—and life in general. *Shouldn't the law protect us?* she wondered. Then the woman realized that the law was only as protective as the nature of those who made and enforced it. She wanted a society that was filled with love. However, love had to be given. It couldn't be demanded or commanded. The gift of love to her was that which played music in the heart. Harmony within, harmony without! As for the law, images seared her mind. *I know the blackness of my soul, and I'm scared to think about what I'm capable of.* Then she imagined a huge set of handcuffs wrapped around a three-dimensional map of the world with all its suffering.

There but for the grace of God... No one is free. Everything I've done or didn't do has affected someone else, and what others have done has affected me. Wherever my conscience is, I feel like I'm being worked like a lump of clay, getting soaked in water, then pushed and turned. I want this change desperately. It's my chance to gain peace. Who wouldn't want to get away from tormenting memories? But it is uncomfortable! What if I can't see it through? I've tried hundreds of ways to help myself, so it must be only in the supernatural sphere where I'll find the answers to my questions. I feel as though I'm just a shell of a person—just a body.

The woman was swept over with feelings of powerlessness, emptiness and meaninglessness, as if her energy had evaporated through her skin. She had heard many stories of people who seemed to have everything, yet who had often wished to obliterate their very existence. Indeed, too many of them had ended their lives. Her shoulders drooped. *How sad!* she thought. The woman knew only too well the dehumanizing process of thinking that life's not worth living. As she scanned her mind to find a reason for this irrational thinking, she suddenly saw inside her soul a dark, driving force that wasn't hers alone. It was a complex inclination common to humanity that seemed to have, at its center, thoughts of doubt and resistance. The courtroom of heaven was strange. Energy drained in some circumstances, and then in others, the energy had intensified force.

I know the flat lethargy of despair, and I know the explosive, burning pain of anger. I'm afraid I won't be able to control the pace when I start to think, act and speak differently. I can't stay the same, and I can't take much more pressure within.

You have heard that it was said, "Love your neighbor and hate your enemy." But I tell you: Love your enemies and pray for those who persecute you, that you may be sons of your Father in heaven (Matthew 5:43-44).

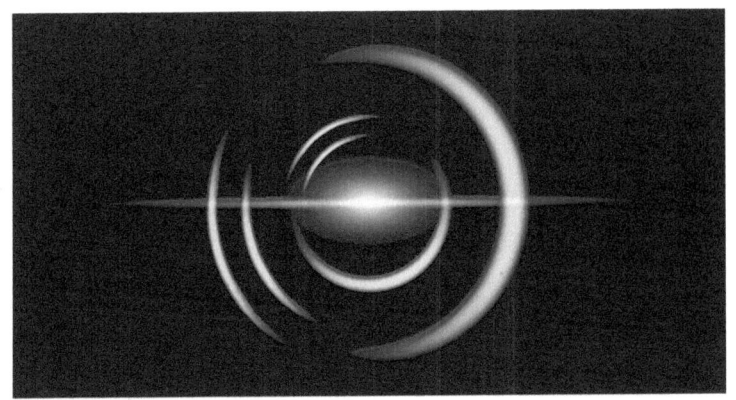

Chapter Six

TO EMBRACE WITH HEART AND MIND

The Sixth Wheel

The woman had understood that God existed in speech, and she had called His name in order to escape the void. It was time for her to evaluate her ideas about Him. So often, to her shame, she had acted to dismantle others' belief in Him, jousting like a gladiator in heated discussions on religion. And simultaneously she hid from any sound argument on His existence.

Why do I do that? Maybe it's a defense mechanism. If I deny that God exists, then my brand of morality is all right. That's putting my head in the sand, isn't it?

She felt foolish. Solely by Light-man's silent, tolerant presence, she was brought to this re-evaluation of her ethics and deeper spiritual values. Ironically, the woman saw a picture of herself, not as the daring gladiator, but as a mere child's toy engaged in the contest of life. Her strategy had been fourfold: 1) to keep out of the way of the mention of God's name and what He stands for. 2) Push down the memories of nightclubs, so alluring in the dark and turning offensive in the morning. 3) Forget the dulled faces. 4) Hide any shame instead of being open to honesty.

After all, she had always paid her debts and taxes, been responsible at work and obeyed the law. Her excuses for avoiding spiritual matters had always been lack of time and interest. Yet surely these were false buffers, set in place so that she would not inquire seriously enough to make internal change.

Things had occupied her, instead of matters of the heart and spirit, and what a poor substitute they were. They were also very risky. Money could vanish overnight. So could her health: It might be fine one minute, but maybe not the next. Relationships failed under stress, and she could see how problems quickly compounded. Her tenuous hold on life could easily snap. The familiar words came to her mind again: *I am a good person. I have worked for my achievement. I have inherent goodness. I ... I ... I.* Self-righteousness and pride had puffed her up like a balloon ready to burst, as she continued to think: *I am respectable.* Her only comparisons were to other people. Human goodness was so affected by circumstances. It was easy to be good if dire need didn't seem to demand desperate actions. Certainly there were great acts of courage and self-denial, yet not even heroes were perfect. The arguments in her head were tiring.

The woman's thoughts turned toward God, or the notion of God, and those thoughts seemed to generate sparks. From now on, she would think of God as if she fully believed in Him. This allowed her to start to see life from His point of view. *How could I have missed the obvious?* she wondered. *Self is not in control!* She had often tossed phrases of the "Why God?" nature out into the universe. However, even when a baby had been born with vast disadvantages, the God who gave attributes to all human beings still gave that child the drive to live and have success. There was indeed an instinct for life. Life! Those who never felt the survival instinct as they scrambled to a safer place could be deluded by the "self-made man myth." But even these people only developed their talents, not manufactured them. As if struck, she knew that the real answer to humanity's questions was God.

The woman recalled something that Solomon wrote: "Who can say, 'I have kept my heart pure; I am clean and without sin'?"

Doing the right thing according to social values did not amount to much when it stood next to the absolute standard of goodness. As if in a replay, she reviewed her life. Strangely, she saw that the imaginations of her mind were often acted upon later, and the results were frequently not righteous. Anger, her unwelcome visitor, would almost inevitably proceed to regrettable words and actions. The woman had walked this path for many years, becoming more and more calloused, so that her attitude became flippant: "I can take God or leave Him," she began to believe. "Just let me be independent." In a strange and new perspective, she saw herself in the context of infinity. It was time to cross a barrier: the acceptance of the existence of God. The "as if God is real" became "He is real." This was not just a mental belief, for in a gigantic opening of her heart and mind together, she yearned for the affectionate relationship with God that others had declared possible. More quietly, she realized that His character was not yet clear to her. The woman wanted to speak to someone for comfort and say: "I feel like I'm standing on a branch that might break. My independence is gone, and I'm on someone else's agenda. In this spiritual sea, although I'm struggling for air, strangely I feel cushioned. To some extent, I'm protected by my detachment. I can see who I've been without God, yet I'm seeing it from the perspective of a new 'me'. I've begun to change at last!"

The woman knew that she could not justify herself in the courtroom of heaven. It was pitiful to even try. No one could earn any favors.

How can I defend myself? My unspoken thoughts and motives are just as much on display as my body. If I could color my wrongs, they would be deep scarlet— like spilt blood. I've lived in a spiritually cold way. I can't understand why I wasn't grateful for what God has given me. Instead, I fired blame at Him. The only way I can see my hard heart being healed is through a love that accepts me as I am and forgives me. That will do it. Then I'll be able to forgive myself and be revived. With the smack of the gavel, the woman jerked to attention. At first she thought the noise was cruel. Then she looked cautiously at the Judge's face. He didn't look cruel, for his mouth was relaxed and his wrinkles were of the favorable kind. Yet there was no mistaking his serious, responsible demeanor toward justice. He was speaking.

"Clerk of the Court, read the charges against the Defendant."

These words beat upon her eardrums:

"The Defendant is charged with every base thought, motive, attitude and action experienced by humanity. The results are family disappointment, self-ambition at work, self-centeredness in relationships, self-righteousness in opinions, reckless waste of gifts and talents and rejection of offered friendships that were not deemed 'good enough.' The Defendant has inflicted wounds that have crippled other people."

Nausea hit the back of her throat. In the past, her center of focus had been on who had hurt her, how and when. The words entered her ears, and she viewed her memories with inner eyes. *What if I died? If hell is real, is that where I will go?* she wondered.

This was the question that changed her life.

What good is it for me to have everything in this life at the expense of losing my soul? Can anything exceed the value of my soul? Being ashamed of someone like Light-man and his stand against evil will only bring shame for not having the courage to stand up for what is right. My soul surely is not only for this world.

What good is it for a man to gain the whole world, yet forfeit his soul? Or what can a man give in exchange for his soul? If anyone is ashamed of me and my words in this adulterous and sinful generation, the Son of Man will be ashamed of him when he comes in his Father's glory with the holy angels. And he said to them, "I tell you the truth, some who are standing here will not taste death before they see the kingdom of God come with power (Mark 8:36-9:1).

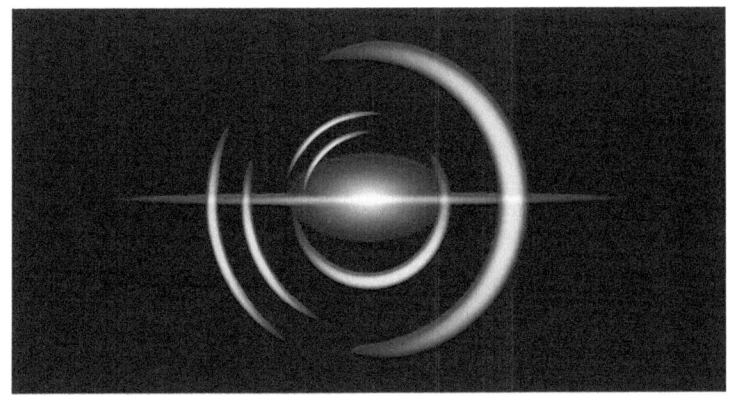

Chapter Seven

ONE WILLING TO DEFEND THE GUILTY

The Seventh Wheel

H er eyes poured tears. The woman stared at the floor and the flaws in her life stared back.

All the anger and despair! Light-man is my only hope. I'm sure only he can thoroughly plead my case. When I'm with him, my thoughts and feelings are so clear and not tangled. I don't know if he'd agree to take charge of my life because there's nothing in it for him to do something like that for me.

The woman mused on this mysterious event. It was like surfing spiritually: She was dumped by unexpected waves, and then floating in the salty froth of freshness and peace. The nausea, which occurred when the charges were read against her, had changed into a faint tingling of anticipation. Memories passed through her mind as if they were on a conveyor belt, so that she was not in a constant state of devastation. Still, a gap existed. She knew that she needed Light-man. Actually doing something about that need was the problem because every change had the risk of unknown consequences. Change was taking place, yet with an accompanying groaning in her being.

Two worlds were being defined as through a mist. Aspects of her life were taking a different shape now in her mind. Sometimes it felt like they were a distortion. At other times, she felt she was being drawn into the right dimension. *I might as well be bread dough with all of this pulling and pushing,* she mused. Hesitantly, she admitted her guilt to herself. There was tremendous opposition present, almost like a rip current, in the courtroom.

This is a waste of time because I'm guilty. I fully deserve a harsh sentence. I'm in real trouble, because it is not only the Judge that I stand before. I now believe in God. He knows I've rejected His creation: myself. It's like a priceless piece of pottery saying to the potter that what he has made is junk. As a mere human, who am I to criticize God? How presumptuous for me to say, "Why have You made me like this?"

Light-man interrupted her inner conversation. She was pleased to be interrupted, especially by the one whom she believed was her supporter, the one with the soothing voice. He read her turmoil and dilemma as she debated whether to give herself totally to change, or stay in familiar straits. He confidently proceeded.

"Woman, listen! Take in as much as you can, for I have to quickly equip you for your case. We only have a few minutes. First of all, the Judge will be looking at your motives. Crimes depend on intent. Different from society as you know it, here in heaven, what you think equals the actual behavior. If you are so angry that you want to kill someone, it is the same as if you murdered that person. The awful reality is that everyone has the potential to do any type of wrong. Everyone has thoughts they are ashamed of. Therefore all are guilty of grievous wrongs, and like you, every single one will have to give an account to the Judge of the way he or she handled the moral difficulties of life."

The woman wondered why she wasn't terrified, because memories were jumping across the screen of her mind. Faces loomed, and then receded, only for another face to take its place. Yet she could hear, see and feel the compassion in the attitude of Light-man toward her. The mere fact he was helping her brought enormous hope. She thought that he was extraordinarily kind: someone willing to defend the guilty. He spoke again.

"Woman, you are in a battle against invisible and powerful, evil enemies. Human beings can't fight against them on their own, for they command armies of dark beings from the heavenly realm."

Vivid, inner pictures of horses, men in armor and opposing armies facing each other in a foggy, smoky dawn, spears slicing the air as in ancient times, seemed so real.

Light-man knew her thoughts and said a puzzling thing. "This war is fought in the mind." At first, her mind would not accept this. Yet she knew if Light-man said it, she needed to try to receive it. Of course, she didn't have to see a horse with her eyes in order to "see" a horse. The word "horse" would show her the appearance of a horse in her imagination. Still, she staggered at the fierceness of the battle that went on in her mind. And then she thought, *So far, so good. I think I understand this.*

Next, Light-man said, "Woman, do not despair or be afraid. I have spiritual armor for you to wear when you stand with me firmly in the instruction I give you. By accepting my ways, your mind will have the protective strength of a helmet, and having faith in my ways will be your shield to protect you from evil. Being right with God is like a breastplate covering your heart and its motives and attitudes. Imagine that truth is the belt on which your spiritual weapons are attached, and you will not be deceived. When your actions agree with me, I give you peace, and you will overcome the things that have crushed you. You have to know truth in order for it to help you. Then, as you take my words as a mighty sword, all evil directed against you by the enemy of your soul will be cut down.

"My dedication is not only to defend individuals, but also to reinstate spiritual territory for humanity. Woman, I cared enough to come to you, and I didn't wait for you to look for me. In fact, I actually chose you so that your life would be productive, with lasting abundance, to replace the desolate years you've been through."

Anxiety left her in a sigh. Astonishingly, here was a man who really knew what her life had been, and who still accepted her. Delightedly, her inner eyes watched as she ran and hopped and skipped and jumped, like a child celebrating. *I'm accepted! I'm acceptable! I have a chance for a better life!* In him, she saw qualities of courage, faithfulness and the highest integrity. He was the gallant rescuer in royal clothes on a brilliant, white steed with an ornamental bridle and saddle.

For God did not send his Son into the world to condemn the world, but to save the world through him (John 3:17).

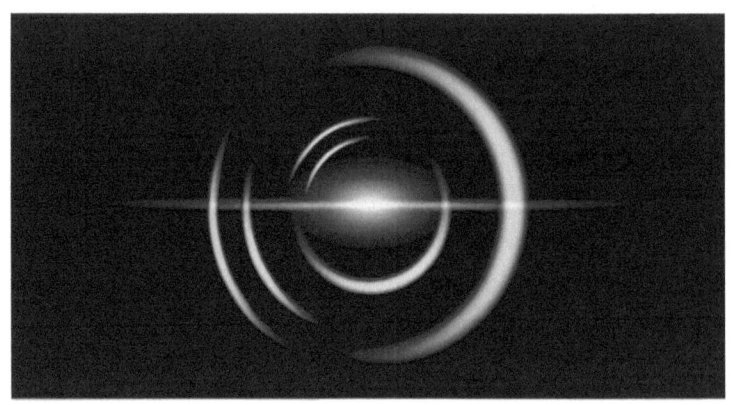

Chapter Eight

CREEPING DREAD, GENTLE HONOR AND HOPE

The Eighth Wheel

W ith a shiver, the woman heard the irritated clearing
of a throat, and the rustle of papers on the left side
of the courtroom. She looked across and straight into the
eyes of Darkness. His eyes then flicked toward Light-man. If
envy and loathing were colors, they would be the venomous
green and slimy yellow of the enemy. It was plain to see that
Darkness desperately desired the clean power of Light-man.
Yet the woman intuitively knew Darkness was only a shabby

copy. After all, Light-man had the type of power that came with honor.

The cost of honor was to deny personal pleasure and comfort for the sake of others' well-being. For that, a person had to be willing to accept great suffering.

The woman knew that she was beginning to change because sheer terror should have filled her as she saw the hideous evil directed at Light-man. As she considered the two of them, the real and the artificial became clear. They both wore expensive robes and were articulate and capable. However, the woman was convinced that only Light-man could be trusted, and she began to suspect that Darkness used threats that were only effective if they were believed. In other words, he relied on lies.

What if all along I've just been fearful of fear? What if those threats were empty and their promises not even going to occur? How much of my life have I wasted running from illusions? Well, the past can't be relived, except in my mind. Now that I've met Light-man, I believe he'll eventually put a stop to this thief who robbed me of the way my life was meant to be. As I am here and learning about the spirit-world, I see that Light-man really can act upon the whole world simultaneously, in order to bring justice and truth. I fear that will be a catastrophic day.

The woman knew that everyone, including herself, had been free to choose goodness or evil, and she had chosen the path away from goodness. She wanted to be punished because she thought that would reduce her guilt. The authorities on the earth hadn't punished her enough in life, so she had formed ways of punishing herself. Guilt! She felt that the word itself was stamped on her forehead, and she felt utterly stupid.

How could I have chosen one like Darkness? I can hardly believe it. This is ridiculous. He's revolting. How I wish I'd never listened to his intimidations!

Light-man had the capacity to speak with perfect timing. He did not immediately address the guilt that had surfaced in her. Yet she was developing hope that he would help her get out of her situation.

He finally spoke. "Woman, this Judge and I are committed to keeping peace and goodness in society. Sadly, it is human nature to defiantly take the one thing denied, in spite of having every other advantage. Just as pure water can't stay pure when it is mixed with mud, there has to be an absolute standard of what is right, to show the difference between right and wrong. This must be a standard beyond corruption. Just consider sunlight for a moment, in all its glorious, pure power. Nothing can be added to it or subtracted from it."

The woman didn't know what Light-man was leading up to. But then he drew from his pocket a leather-bound book that had his name on it. She assumed that it contained his credentials, and as she opened it, she expected to see a list of his achievements, perhaps with a well-organized theory of his methods. Instead, it was like a love letter, addressed to interested readers. A timeless quality exuded from the words on these pages, as if he had always existed and would always exist.

The book was interconnected and interwoven like wool in a multicolored jumper, yet with phenomenal cohesion. It seemed beyond reason that any person or collection of people could have assembled it. Intuitively, she knew that the book was priceless, and she held it delicately in the palms of her hands. A cry pressed her face, for she had nothing to give him in return. The more he was kind, the more she wanted to hide. No one had treated her with this kind of softness. He seemed to believe in her.

Many philosophies had passed through the woman's eyes over time. Only this one took hold. In it, she saw the world's most heroic man, masterful beyond humanity's scope. He was revolutionary, able to conquer through non-violence, to triumph over evil by goodness. In the book, she read of Light-man: "My mission is to redeem people who have been bought as pawns by an unscrupulous fiend. I value and cherish the life placed in each one. The spiritually poor can have hope."

Remorse pulled the corners of her mouth downward, and tears pricked her eyes. The realization that she had listened to, condoned and perpetuated malicious rumors against him, felt like a slap with its stinging awareness. Inside her head the words bounced, as if they were in an echo chamber: *You're to blame for all that's happened. You carry trouble wherever you go.* The thoughts weren't new, and she had often assumed God wanted her to feel guilty in this way. She had denigrated God, and so it seemed logical that He would reprimand her.

Having met Light-man, she knew that uncomplicated, non-manipulative goodness could exist. She began to see the answer to her confusion and meaninglessness in life. Those bases for her life had only produced understanding that was built with a serious error in its foundation. When that happened in a building, the error intensified with each level built above it, until it teetered and even fell. A sharp slice of truth like light entered her thoughts.

If I do what Light-man says, my life will be as solid as a rock, able to withstand the storms of life. It's clear to me that all I do, whether for good or otherwise, will come out in the end. He is the only one who is intent on helping me. He can show me how to fix the foundations of my understanding.

Light-man personified truth, and yet this truth could be both a challenge and a choice. He placed these before her.

"Woman, truth brings light and clarity to mental blindness and confusion. When you know the facts, you can tackle any problem because truth is a plumb line for the soul, just as an actual plumb line prevents errors in a building. It is now up to you whether you will commit to seeking and loving truth, or stay as you are. I must know if you choose to value your life and live within guidelines that promote it. The familiar, crooked path will only end in tragedy. Your life has hit rock bottom; you have lost your family, friends, career and property. In fact, only a miracle can erase your past and give you a clean start. Remember, even pretending not to make a decision is still a decision."

Put in these terms, the choice seemed straightforward, and she was mystified that she had taken so long to see it. Light-man was not the usual kind of man. He was protective of her, like a friend who had seen her harassed by life. She wasn't just a case in which he gave her legal counsel. If that were so, his words alone would have been severe. Instead he spoke with firm gentleness, offering to help her. Yet he wanted her commitment, too. The exchange seemed grossly lopsided. *He has everything. What can I possibly give?* she wondered. Then she realized that pledging her affection and obedience would at least be something.

The woman spoke to Light-man: "Yes! I want to be different. Others say you're a refuge. Without you, I have no real hope, and I can't change myself. I'll do what you say and put my total trust in you. I'll tell you everything."

Words tumbled through her mouth, and tears washed her eyes. It was pointless trying to hold them back, although the pain tempted her to do so. Then there was ease. All her guilt and shame was dissolved by his kindness. She knew that she could now stand in the presence of the Judge as a new person.

The woman had thought that her problems in her life had come from other people. Yet in this clarity, she understood that her wrongs had been against a moral plumb line. Light-man had those high attributes. She was glad that her guilt had dissolved, but the charges still stood. They had to be faced. She felt so low having to be helped by the one she'd first held in contempt.

"Light-man, will you represent me and be my Advocate, despite all I've done?" she asked hesitantly.

At first, the woman was afraid to look into his eyes, for she didn't want to see him condemn or reject her. Nevertheless, she had to know. His look was a mixture of authority and penetrating kindness, without any trace of desiring retribution. As Light-man glanced across the courtroom, she saw his steely determination to fight to prevent Darkness from snatching her freedom. At this point, she knew that Light-man was her Advocate.

Simultaneously, the one who the woman had called Darkness identified himself. He was the Accuser. He shot icy, clipped words against her quietly, hoping the Judge would not hear.

"You're a fool! A gullible fool! I'll get even with you! You'll be sorry, really sorry, for listening to that naïve morals campaigner! He hasn't got a hope against me! If you thought you suffered before, that was nothing! I'll completely destroy you. I'll drive you crazy!"

Involuntarily she shook, as she looked at the film of hate over his eyes. She realized she was merely an object in his view to be possessed: a pawn in the dire game he played against her Advocate.

For our struggle is not against flesh and blood, but against the rulers, against the authorities, against the powers of this dark world and against the spiritual forces of evil in the heavenly realms (Ephesians 6:12).

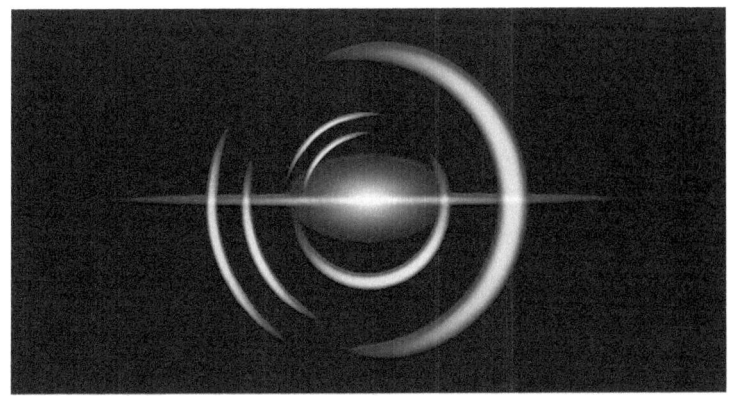

Chapter Nine

THE MYSTERIOUS, HORRIFIC EXECUTION

Wheel Within the Wheels

The woman's Advocate said that he could open doors that no one could shut, and shut doors that no one could open. She saw that his relationship with the Judge was completely ethical and would play a major role in the defeat of every false charge against her. Though she hoped for vindication, she could not have conceived how it would occur. It was as far from comprehension as trying to fit the planets into the space of the earth. There was no comparison in humanity's history.

Although she was awake, her mind felt in a twist to reconcile how she could be present in this extraordinary event.

A depiction of a horrific execution upon her Advocate seared her mind. Incongruously, within a moment, she was talking with him again. The death she had just seen had not stopped his existence. By a mysterious and what could only be divine transaction, she watched a replay on the screen of her mind. A ransom was paid by the blood-sacrifice of her Advocate: his life was given instead of hers. His virtue passed to her, and her guilt flooded back into him, her body acting like a membrane. The Judge! What grief she saw in his face! Pain seemed to implode his chest in the anguish of loss as he watched.

The woman knew that her Advocate's suffering had been as much for anyone else as for her. Sickeningly, he was just a mass of blood, unrecognizable by the end of the torture. But as he returned to life in that moment, her Advocate was triumphant. Unfortunately, she felt detached from the extreme violence, and intuitively wanted to grasp the agony—to feel the love that birthed it. Yet the Advocate's stately disposition directed her to the future.

The woman still responded. She felt deep remorse for her wrongs, and the gaping wound in her heart was mended. Peace beyond understanding had arrived. In another flash of thought, she glimpsed the fantastic comparison of the God of the universe being lovingly conscious of humanity, individual by individual.

"I am a new person. How can I ever explain this exchange? I have a taste of faith: believing without tangible facts."

Her Advocate replied, "Eternity is set in your heart. Everything was made beautiful in creation. The significance of all that is between the beginning and the end is too much to grasp at this time. There is nothing better for you than to be happy and do good while you live. Eat and drink, and find satisfaction in all your labor, with reverence to God, for these are his gifts."

The word "eternity" held her attention in the mystery of it. She assumed that God had made her aware of eternity so that she would better know how to be reverent toward Him. This moving situation—being on trial in the courtroom of heaven—was actually the breakthrough for which she had yearned.

"My Advocate, I give you my will as well as my love and obedience, for I desire this peace in my mortal life as well as in Heaven."

Surprisingly he responded, "I have petitioned the Judge for you. You are made free and this case is finished."

Usually, a person is presumed innocent until proven guilty. But the woman knew that she was actually guilty, then tried and found innocent. By this justice, it was as if her crimes had never existed.

Since the children have flesh and blood, he too shared in their humanity so that by his death he might destroy him who holds the power of death—that is, the devil—and free those who all their lives were held in slavery by their fear of death (Hebrews 2:14-15).

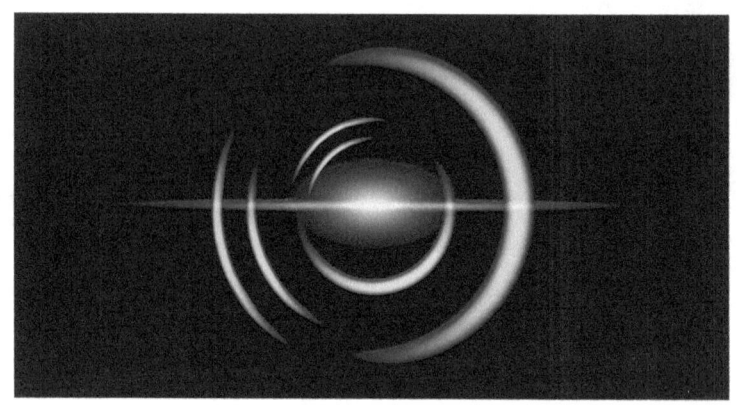

Chapter Ten

BEATING THE TUG OF VACILLATIONS

The Ninth Wheel

Witnessing the execution and restoration of her Advocate was inexplicable, yet strangely uplifting. Her peace fractured briefly, as if a sharp rock hit window glass. Again, the barrage of harassing words echoed within her mind and reverberated around her. She instantly recognized their source: the Accuser.

Why is he so intent on destroying me? His outrage is extreme. Aren't I the one who has suffered through my wrong choices? I guess he instigated them, anyway. This is too much. There must be more to it.

Then her thoughts veered away from the Accuser's attack, and they became an attack on herself:

No! My life isn't different. Everything's just as difficult. How can I escape from my mental prison? The book says that being guilty of one crime is as good as being guilty of every crime, and I have a multitude of them. My problems are mocking me, tempting me to give up.

However, this time, the woman quickly recovered as she remembered her Advocate. He had said he would help her in the process of change. It was clear that the Accuser had intended to trap her and wreck her hopes. Yet knowing she was no longer in this battle alone strengthened her. Legal professionals usually confined themselves to flat facts. Her Advocate was extraordinary in that he was also interested in her mental and emotional well-being. It was comforting how her Advocate's words could sound both firm and soft at the same time.

Her Advocate said: "Woman, you are making progress, so don't be discouraged. You fought back in the battle in your mind just then. It is time to let go of all fear, for I will fight your case. Success comes by taking possession of your legal rights. Nevertheless, I must be absolutely certain of your commitment to change."

He wanted her to realize that change would not be instant. She would get up and fall down, get up and fall down, and get back up again to overcome her problems in relation to not just one issue, but multiple issues. Each time she succeeded, hope would be more vigorously fanned to life. She had to assimilate right information in order to form right thinking.

The Advocate spoke again: "Woman, this breaks through the traps that are set in your mind, traps that are just as brutal as animal traps. The power to change is in the amount of insight, like light, that can penetrate your blind spots where darkness resides. Again I say, without the inner embrace of the truth, there will be no change."

His words had a cleansing effect. The woman felt clean, as if she had bathed in a crystal creek. Her mind became clear. She thought peace, and peace filled her mind and emotions. Her Advocate had not asked anything in return for the pain he had endured to secure her freedom. She wanted to know him more deeply.

Suddenly she heard the Judge speak to the clerk: "Read the charges once again to the Court."

This was the man who would determine her fate. She concentrated on every fine movement of his facial muscles for a clue to his reactions. Surprisingly, he seemed not to be wearied by the stream of criminals who were presented to him each day. It was also clear that he was not likely to be manipulated or controlled by them. Many professionals pretended hard objectivity, but he did not use that mechanical screen. She felt confident he would treat her sympathetically on the facts. It appeared that her Advocate had a harmonious relationship with the Judge, so she hoped for mercy.

The Clerk of the Court read the charges as instructed: "The defendant is charged with every base thought, motive, attitude and action experienced by humanity. The results are disappointment of parents, self-ambition at work, self-centeredness in relationships, self-righteousness in opinions, reckless waste of gifts and talents and the rejection of offered friendships that were classed as 'not good enough.' The Defendant has inflicted wounds that have crippled people."

Everyone knew why she was there and what she had done: It was a public display that should have been shameful. Yet the woman felt an upsurge of gratitude. Her life had been going downhill until she met Light-man, who was now her Advocate. Even if this was her only reason for being in the courtroom of heaven, she knew that at least he loved her soul enough to rescue and defend her.

In a careful, probing tone, the Judge asked: "How do you plead?"

The Judge did not choose to sit behind the bench but rather in a dark brown, leather armchair with one armrest fitted with a flat surface for writing notes. There was a spotlight over this surface, so that the light did not directly hit his face. This helped the woman not to feel as self-conscious, and it softened the atmosphere. She had expected that he would sit on a platform, requiring her to look up at him. Had that been the case, she was sure that inferiority and insecurity would have filled her mind. There were frequent small points like these that gave her the experience of thankfulness. Still, the woman felt her plight with numbness. Her Advocate quickly and quietly instructed her.

"Enter a plea of 'Not Guilty' on the grounds that a verdict of 'Innocent' on these charges has already been made. This is an illegal retrial, for you were made free when I petitioned the Judge for you on the basis that you have given me charge of your life."

The woman saw her true legal position and said in a firm voice, "Not guilty, Your Honor."

The Judge spoke watchfully, "Innocence has been put on trial before, and the case will proceed." The Judge alluded to her Advocate's sacrificial death: his life for hers. He had done no wrong, and only perfect innocence could have allowed him to pass through death and survive to live again. At this point, the woman wondered, *I'm the one facing trial, yet could it be that the one actually under scrutiny is my Advocate and all he stands for?*

> *"If I said something wrong," Jesus replied, "testify as to what is wrong. But if I spoke the truth, why did you strike me?" (John 18:23)*

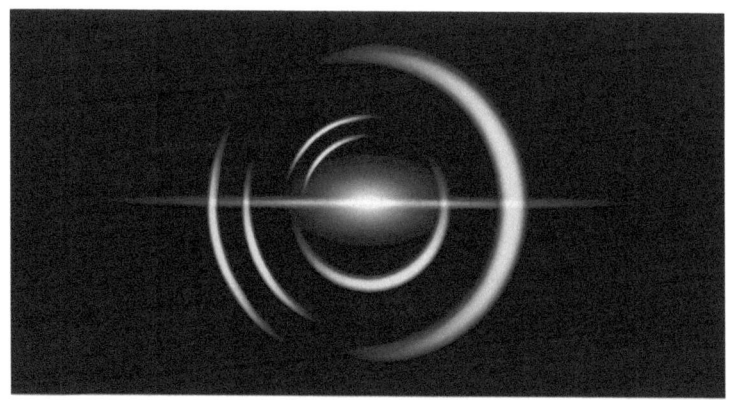

Chapter Eleven

FRIENDS AND AN ENEMY OF THE SOUL

The Tenth Wheel

It was time for the Judge to call for the witnesses. He did this with a minimum of words. In this ethereal place, the only eyewitnesses able to speak in the courtroom of heaven were her Advocate and the Accuser. The woman's jaw tightened and her lips were white, pressed together. It was one thing to believe the words of her Advocate, yet until the case was finished, there were no guarantees. Who could tell what the Accuser might say? The woman had so many new thoughts and feelings that she often lost alertness to the other dynamics taking place in the courtroom. When her Advocate spoke, it almost came as an interruption.

Her Advocate took his oath on the Bible, "I swear by Almighty God that the evidence I give will be the truth, the whole truth and nothing but the truth."

Defiantly, the Accuser chose his affirmation: "I do solemnly and sincerely and truly declare and affirm that the evidence I give shall be the truth, the whole truth and nothing but the truth."

His voice was strained—his throat tight with aggravation. Barely in control, with his upper lip pulled away from his teeth and his nostrils wide, he looked like an unbroken horse fighting its master. Because the Accuser's attention was focused on the Judge, the woman was able to glance furtively at him. She saw that his robes were stretching the decorum of the Court in their extravagance, and his fingers were covered with expensive, though ugly, jewelry. The edges of his robes were dirty, as were his fingernails, and his teeth were yellowed and decaying.

She thought, *He's not what he claims to be, and he's not worthy to stand in this Court. What's the Judge looking for? He's already said, 'Innocence has been put on trial before,' and that implies that he thinks I'm innocent.*

There was a look of intent on the Judge's face—a look that said, "No nonsense will be tolerated."

The Judge then spoke with quiet strength: "What documentary evidence does each of you tender?"

Her Advocate simply tendered a Contract of Adoption, while the Accuser set forth a flurry with medical, psychiatric and financial reports.

To present the woman's case, her Advocate needed to examine certain facts of her life in order to make sense of them. He requested a recess. In his chambers, he elaborated on the notion of "intent" and how responsibility could be diminished. This was an opportunity for the woman to understand some legal principles that would affect her case.

"Woman, the emotional contents of the heart are hidden. Most people want facts—to see with their eyes before believing that certain information is true. However, many true things in everyday life are accepted even though they remain unseen. Surgeons cannot dissect the mind— only the brain. Likewise, the conscience cannot be put under a literal microscope. Unfortunately, in life you have often not seen the right and true thing to do. Let me explain further.

"Your personality is like a gigantic filing cabinet in which all events, happy or traumatic, are stored. Some of these are almost fossilized, having been compressed throughout your genetic history, even back to Adam, so to speak. So you do some of the things your parents did; they did what their parents did, and so on. You've probably wondered why you do these things because there is no apparent reason. It is as if you don't see through your own eyes because you are filtering out vital information. Then, how you process and interpret what is happening to you isn't real.

"What I'm describing is distortion. You often react to triggers from inside rather than from outside. You are not even aware of the effects. That is how you can be manipulated and controlled."

The woman absorbed his words as a thirsty sponge. Two conditions in particular were affecting her. First, it was as if her essence had come out of a dormant state. Second, it was obvious to her that she needed to reeducate her memory and habits. In this Court, she had these charges to face. Yet this time, it was different, for she knew her innocence, and therefore the law could not hold her. This tangle in her mind was already being straightened out by truth. It was the way to her inner freedom. She felt confident, as if an archer had shot an arrow to the center of its target. Something else was happening, however. Her personal history, or even the effects of society, could not fully explain how she had sunk to such a state of desolation before this supernatural event.

Her Advocate seemed pleased that she was beginning to work with the information he had given her:

"Woman, you must know the tactics of the Accuser, who is causing your adversity. He plagues you with lies and smokescreens, and is out to destroy as much of your life as he can. Like a snake in the grass, he comes by stealth and surprise. By his arrogant and blatant pride, he aims to destroy even the most saintly. The Accuser actually hides under the guise of being superior in intellect and talent. However, he stole, murdered and destroyed the quality of life for countless people in his quest for success. His word is worthless. Listen, woman! Embrace truth, for only truth exposes lies."

When her Advocate said this, the woman saw that absolute standards were indispensable. She actually pictured the brilliance of gold purified by extreme heat. Absolute meant God.

"Yes!" It was an "Ah-ha!" moment for her. Human thinking could not compare to the thoughts of the Creator of humanity. As the earth turned on its axis amid the galaxies, she saw a parallel: Society was held together by truth. This brought a delighted smile to her Advocate's face. She was amazed how he knew what she was thinking. If the Accuser was the counterfeit, could her Advocate be the pure standard? He was unpretentious yet authoritative, kind yet strong. To put it in a word, he was able.

"Woman, it is God who is always in every place present, all knowing and all-powerful. You've seen how error stunted your understanding in every facet of life. Do you now see that reason simply cannot answer life's problems? You need to believe—beyond analyzing and debating—that God is loving."

Instinctively, she knew he was right; yet she still had to ask:

"How do I connect the expanse between my thinking and my emotions? I don't want to settle for an understanding that doesn't feel true. My desire is to have spirited convictions like yours."

Her Advocate replied: "Let us focus on this trial first. The right mind/emotion process has begun and will keep operating if you follow my instructions, even when you are not consciously doing so. Now! Your past is dead, and every time you feel the impulse to give it life in your thoughts, reactions or actions, adamantly say, 'This is a dead issue.' The attacks on your mind won't cease just because you know the truth. It is how you fight each attack that counts. Even in this courtroom, the enemy of your soul waits for opportunities. Do you see? Your past has no power over you unless you keep it alive.

"Let's backtrack. There are two worlds—two opposing forces. Invisible forces cannot be tested or proved by science, which relies on reason, and obviously, you can't agree with or follow opposing sides. The key to being acquitted is by faith. Your mind might be arguing one way, and your conscience will be telling you to go the other way. Just think of striking a match. Light always dominates darkness. Darkness cannot quench light. Follow your conscience in matters of right and wrong, rather than your mind, which will try to excuse what is wrong."

At this point, she felt at ease, so different from her usual emotional state. That was progress. It made her goals in life appear more reachable. However, she wondered what kind of attack would come against her next.

Her Advocate continued: "Remember your experience when you figuratively saw the supernatural exchange of my life for yours? That event removed the destructive power of your past, and your spirit was awakened as if reborn. My strength and ability can now help you to live to your full capacity. However, I repeat, it is important to keep up the words of my book."

Therefore, there is now no condemnation for those who are in Christ Jesus, because through Christ Jesus the law of the Spirit of life set me free from the law of sin and death. For what the law was powerless to do in that it was weakened by the sinful nature, God did by sending his own Son in the likeness of sinful man to be a sin offering. And so he condemned sin in sinful man, in order that the righteous requirements of the law might be fully met in us, who do not live according to the sinful nature but according to the Spirit (Romans 8:1-4).

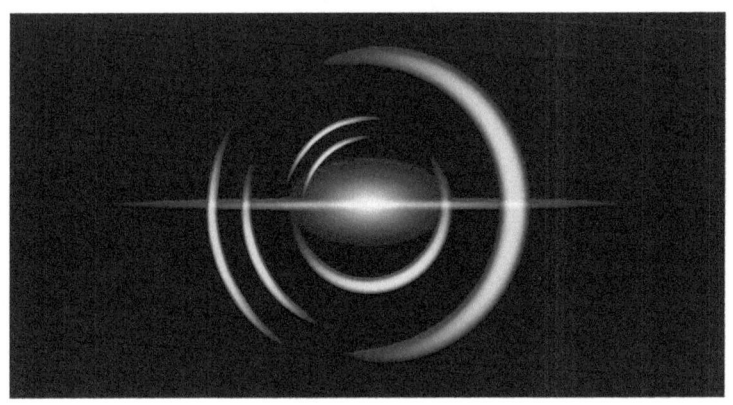

Chapter Twelve

ESCAPE FROM THE VICE'S GRIP

The Eleventh Wheel

Peace is often fragile, and it splinters easily. The woman sustained a reverberating jolt when her Advocate said, "Forgive those who have hurt you." A surge of resentment, like a hot mud pool, bubbled inside her temples. In the driving turbulence of that moment, she completely forgot her immense gratitude to the boy who had forgiven her.

Vehemently she said: "Why should I? People who don't even care have abused me. My life has been a series of injustices. Surely I'm justified to blame and hate those who hurt me! Forgiveness is too difficult!"

She knew that bitterness was really a monkey on her back and that most of the time the other person wasn't even aware of what she was feeling. It was logical to chase those feelings away, yet somehow she wanted to hang on to them.

Her Advocate was undeterred by her protest, dispensing his advice like distasteful medicine: "Woman, there is a self-preserving aspect to forgiveness. It is such an important ingredient to your well-being, but only you can decide to act on my advice. Just because you forgive someone else, the other person may not offer forgiveness to you—and it cannot be demanded. Face your emotions and the thoughts and attitudes that back them, for this will minimize the damage to you. Yes! There is unfairness, but it is counterproductive to question why others have escaped adversity."

The woman knew that she had made assumptions about the motives and actions of others, and that this process had achieved little. She decided that in the future she would put herself in the shoes of the other person, and through this process, she would be able to recognize that everyone had problems. But she still wanted to be understood, and momentarily she felt gripped in a vice of self-pity and self-justification. Then subdued, she recognized how that vice had immobilized her potential for happiness.

Her Advocate knew the subject of forgiveness well. "Woman, for the firm stand I take, you may be angry with me. Although I have not created your anger, you may start by forgiving me for any hurt you may feel." She realized it was unnecessary to do so and relaxed a little. Then unexpected, ghostly faces appeared in her memory, and a wave of ugly emotion again swept her off balance. Her Advocate drew her toward forgiveness again. He was a lifesaver. Every time she wanted to drown in her past, he threw her a line.

"Woman, what does bitterness achieve? Believing that you are right will not alleviate the pain of your experiences. It will not bring you out of the victim mentality because you are repeatedly reliving trauma. The fury inside gets bigger, traveling with you everywhere and bursting without warning, only to refill again. It is true that your forgiveness of someone may not bring a positive change in the treatment you receive. Yet there is always the possibility of resolution. Forgiveness is a process, and resentment will eventually shrink to nothing."

This caught her attention.

"By forgiving, you will have more space within for pleasant emotions and the ability to break out of the circles of the past."

What he said made good sense, and so she was willing to put his advice into practice. After unjust treatment, she would decide to forgive any resulting emotional trouble. The face of the boy from her past lit her imagination with his smile of rich peace and consent.

Her Advocate continued: "Woman, you have gained ground in the areas of leaving your past behind and embracing forgiveness. You understand the power of truth, and you have also learned that not all thoughts in your mind are your own thoughts. Now, it is very important that you take control of the words you speak. You think that others can read your mind, that they can see your low self-esteem, embarrassment and feelings of foolishness. They cannot, just as you cannot see their fears and doubts. You often perceive them as being superior and yourself as inferior. Until your words disclose your state of mind, no one really knows what you are thinking. Even body language, which can be so helpful in reading people's reactions, is only a general guide. Overwrite your painful memories with new experiences by filling your mind with the new way of perceiving who you are—one who has been set free from internal imprisonment.

"Speak of yourself accordingly: 'I am set free from all that has held me in chains.' Build a bridge between how you are today and how you will be tomorrow by expecting better results. The realm of the spirit will far exceed your natural imagination. Nonetheless, look for steady growth, not instant perfection. Do not think of yourself as unchangeable, for I am with you to comfort and strengthen you."

Her Advocate had made the process of change sound so simple. She simply had to flip a switch and change her outlook from negative to positive. This switch allowed him to help her. In his book, he had written, "Happy are you when you put my words into practice for it is the cake that proves the recipe." The woman thought of all the phenomenal things she had learned in the courtroom of heaven. Before knowing her Advocate, she had been like an out-of-focus photograph. As her

Advocate talked, she began to see that her self-image could fuse with her new identity. The destructive memories could be detached, and it was up to her to prevent them from being re-energized. Her Advocate had made dramatic changes, almost as if he had drawn her from an underground passage.

> He replied, "*Blessed rather are those who hear the word of God and obey it*" (*Luke 11:28*).

Chapter Thirteen

ONE INDIVIDUAL IN THE CONTEXT OF INFINITY

The Twelfth Wheel

The Court Recess was over. The Judge entered the courtroom with definite steps. He didn't wear his usual courtroom robes and wig. Significantly, he wore a ring that could be used for making seals of certain documents. His nationality was mysterious, and the woman thought he could be claimed as a father by many races. *Yes!* thought the woman. *He seems fatherly, but not the out-of-date kind of father. I like his eyes the most. They're so fascinating, with clear, pure facets, just like a diamond.*

The Judge called the Accuser to address the court first. The woman had discovered that, because this was the courtroom of heaven, the prosecutor and the defense counsel were also witnesses. Therefore, it was to transpire that the Advocate, the Accuser and the Defendant were on trial in different ways. In supercilious tones, the Accuser jabbed his words at several targets:

"Judge, the defendant is guilty, a liar and a loser in life, and is beyond rehabilitation. Just look at her medical, psychiatric and financial reports! She's unstable. You can't believe a word she says. The Defendant has had the opportunity to advance in life, to become wealthy and powerful. However, she failed. She failed, Judge! The Defendant knows that everything in those reports is true. She's guilty! No doubt about it! She'll never be a success at anything: She never would be, never could be and never will be. All I can see is poor character, nastiness, meanness and selfishness. The Defendant's life is a drain on society and not worth living anyway."

The woman sagged both outwardly and inwardly. She could recall that she had accepted enticements to wealth, success and power in her before-life. In those days, she had surrendered to temptations, but she was tormented whether she acted upon them or not. The Accuser had arranged these enticements, with a sting, she was sure. In his animated attack, the Accuser continued:

"Judge, you can see through this façade, and I recommend that you apply a severe sentence for the misery the Defendant has caused. It is pathetic for her to hide behind this Advocate, pretending to be innocent. The Advocate is a sickly do-gooder, taking on this hopeless case. Belief in goodness is a joke. There's not much good happening in the human race, is there, Judge? Now Judge, I want my status and power to be made equal with yours. I'll make sure you get good publicity if you decide in my favor."

The woman heard a sneer in the Accuser's words. His face buckled at his nose and mouth to form the intonations. It wasn't only the sound that was debased. He was contemptuous of the Judge's office. *If only hindsight could be foresight*, she thought. How could someone so blatantly rebellious have seduced her into believing him? He had always denigrated her, and she had become increasingly blind in spirit and mind.

She thought, *He made my body sick, and he wrecked my relationships, too. Now I see how he hides behind his intellect and cultural pursuits. All the garb of success and power can't cover his hatred for those who fall for his lies. Of course, he hates those who are wise to him even more. The Accuser thinks everyone will give in to him—and too many do. Although I don't like to see it, I'm learning to recognize the trademarks of the Accuser's degenerate nature. It's terrifying to think what would have happened to me if my Advocate hadn't opened the eyes of my soul.*

The Judge then called her Advocate in a tone similar to the one used with the Accuser. The woman recognized the fact that there would be no favoritism. The Judge was just and would not allow any reason for ann claim of bias ever to be made against him. However, at this point, she found his attitude toward her inscrutable. No doubt he heard the contempt in the Accuser's voice. He would also have read the reports tabled by the Accuser, which were certainly true at the time they were written. The woman spoke softly so that no one could hear:

"Please God! Don't let the Judge be affected by these reports. They're dreadful, but I'm different now."

Her Advocate spoke respectfully and authoritatively. The woman noticed again that peculiar whispering echo behind his words—that seashell sound. There was a mighty power in her Advocate.

"Your Eminence, I have taken my oath on the ultimate declaration of truth before Almighty God. My words are not just lip service. In all sincerity, I align my life with God. This enables me to be a rescuer and defender of the oppressed, and to lead them step-by-step into a new life.

"The affirmation taken by the Accuser is significant, but it is merely a standard based on variable human capacities. The Defendant is innocent. Emphatically, the past of this person is dead. Yes! The Defendant was guilty by association at one time. However, she was acquitted. All have contravened their consciences in some way. No new evidence has come forth, and information from any previous court hearing must be ruled as inadmissible. Significantly, no criminal record can be produced. I have taken special interest in this Defendant and have assumed Legal Guardianship of her life. The Contract of Adoption was tendered as evidence at the commencement of this trial.

"Your Eminence, in summary, I ask that you please find the Defendant to be innocent."

The woman felt dizzy with the rhapsody of knowing that her Advocate was her Legal Guardian. The room seemed to spin for a moment. Returning to alertness, she watched her

Advocate address the Court. The contrast between him and the Accuser was unmistakable. Her Advocate spoke with legal precision, as if a sword were slicing through the lies of the Accuser. She briefly mused on her strange adventure. Her Advocate clearly had certain objectives: to understand and defend her, and to obtain her release. He hadn't spoken of himself except to guide her to the leather-bound book. But even then, he had given her a choice. She could make the effort to read it, or she could just draw help from him in the immediate crisis and then neglect any ongoing relationship. She was humbled by his selflessness.

The Judge then spoke. "What do you say, Defendant?"

Although his words were few, the Judge sounded genuinely willing to listen, almost as if he had not made a final decision. Rarely had she been made to feel significant in her lifetime. In such an elevated court, she had a weird glimpse of perspective: one individual in the context of infinity.

The woman wondered, *What does this Judge think of me? I was guilty of everything in those reports. Yet everyone has done wrong—everyone except, perhaps, my Advocate. I'm convinced I've been made innocent.*

But will this Judge believe it? The Accuser is very persuasive, and he has evidence if it is ruled admissible. I know so little about the Judge. His silence somewhat unnerves me. Of course, he can't speak until all the evidence is presented. How I wish I knew what he is thinking. I hope he believes in rehabilitation, not punishment for its own sake.

The atmosphere felt tense. The woman had scarcely taken in the details of the courtroom, because she had been preoccupied with peering into the faces affecting her fate. Their expressions were her barometer and compass. In a slight distraction, she looked around. The courtroom did not appear to be the place in heaven where angels sang. This was serious business. The presence of her Advocate provided her with safety that she otherwise would not have known. When she had first met him, she had called him Light-man. That name now gained an unexpected relevance. She saw him like a lighthouse, shining on calm nights as well as in storms: a friend for all weather. She knew the storms in her past had been settled, yet the storms in her future would be of a totally different kind. Storms would not cease—they would just be different.

The woman's thoughts ran at a pace of thousands per minute. The Judge had asked her to speak, and he was waiting patiently. She felt that she needed more time to prepare herself emotionally. Then from the depths of her mind, she drew upon some expressions of her Advocate: "Do not be afraid for I hold you with my hand. I will not fail or abandon you. Do not to be discouraged in the process of the case, for I will see it through to completion. Justice will be served in this courtroom of heaven. Stand still, and see how I will save you from the Accuser."

It was time to make her statement.

"Your Honor, the Accuser told me that I could only scrape through life using a crutch. The truth is, I needed crutches when I was tormented and oppressed by him. Now I vigorously chase away his mind-manipulations. I threw out my crutches when I turned away from the Accuser's control, and I have unequivocally aligned my life with my Advocate: a man of real strength. I thought I had chosen to change. Now it is clear that he had observed me first and initiated the process.

"My help has come externally. My first step was to believe there is a God. Then I believed in God. Then I developed loving affection for Him. The Creator is beyond the visible creation, and I see that my thoughts, my ability to reason, my purest emotions and the conscience that sustains my life all originated in him. I have the hope that I will exist in the unseen, beyond life in my body.

"My relationship with the Advocate has given me the opportunity to understand truth and goodness, and to believe I am capable of extraordinary achievements with his help. My Advocate is perfect in his expression of love for suffering humanity. He warns people that evil has punishment—that goodness and evil cannot mix. If white is not contrasted with black, then everything is gray. I have made the decision to follow the way of goodness. Now I meditate on the words he speaks and writes. My mental and emotional confusion and erratic behavior have gone. Your Honor, I know from experience that humanity is selfish, always looking after its personal needs first. But because of the mysterious exchange between my Advocate and myself, I find that I am able to love others, with or without reward. It is as if I have eyes that see the unseen solution, instead of the seen problem. Then the unseen solution comes into operation for my eyes to see visibly. I realize that I could never have won with the Accuser, although he promises the world. Any acceptance of his promises is a trap with iron jaws that clamp and maim mercilessly."

Silently the woman heard the voices of people from her past. She continued: "It's not enough just to say, 'It was not my fault because I was simply corrupted by the corruptible one.' Yes! I was responsible for my own wicked thoughts, words and actions. However, I now see that one tactic of the Accuser was to keep me in guilt— never free. No! I'm no longer his prey. My Advocate provided the way of escape by being my substitute. That fact is my armor."

The purpose of her Advocate's intense and careful instruction became apparent. Her case was built on the fact that "innocence was on trial." Essentially, she had to believe this beyond doubt because doubt would reactivate her guilt. Confidently she said, "Your Honor, I truly am innocent." The woman was exhilarated by the eloquence of her statement. She had stood in this noble court and spoken without inferiority, guilt or shame. She was not speaking from reason only. The utter conviction of the truth of her words was that for which she had longed. Her central belief had been established like a rock cemented into a wall: "I'm a winner—no longer a loser. Life's a commodity to spend, and I won't waste it from this point on."

What happened next completely astounded the court.

Therefore, if anyone is in Christ, he is a new creation; the old has gone, the new has come! (2 Corinthians 5:17)

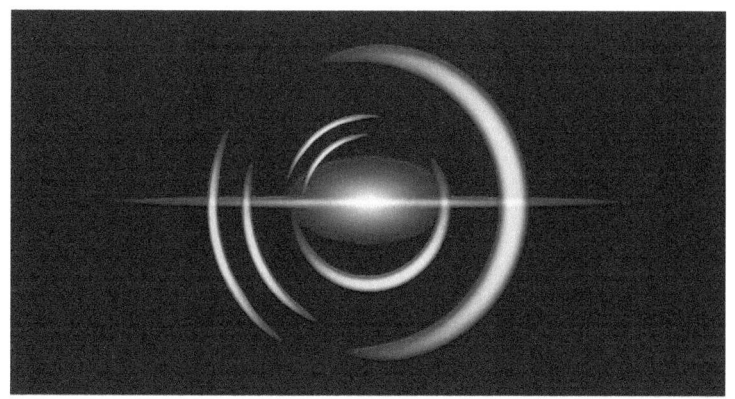

Chapter Fourteen

DIVINE JUSTICE

The Thirteenth Wheel

In a grand advance, the woman's Advocate made a cross-claim: "Herewith, I charge the Accuser with perjury, false accusation, stalking, mental cruelty, slander, attempted murder and theft. The Accuser infuses doubt by questioning whether anyone acts honorably, trying to discredit the case for the Defense, in his maneuver for personal gain."

As the Advocate continued, his words had extraordinary, penetrating command. Momentarily, slivers of light appeared to flash around his head and from every gesture of his arms and hands. His eyes gleamed, from within, with passion for divine justice. She had never seen this type of fierce, pure supremacy.

He continued: "Truth is the key to this case, and I am its witness. It is a case of goodness versus evil. The evil of the Accuser is real. Brainwashing and manipulation of the Defendant caused emotional damage by inducing guilt, shame and inferiority. The attacks to destroy her peace have been relentless as he has set obstructions, temptations and persecution in her path. The contentious and foolish arguments of the Accuser are worthless.

"How can the testimony of the Accuser be believed? I know him to be destitute of truthfulness and a master of lies. He is murderous in deception. By abusing the function of this court, he wants to destroy the reputation and identity of this Defendant. Many do not see or believe that evil motivations are in him.

"Evil is not just a fantasy that has been made into legends. The Accuser gloats over disaster and cannot go unpunished. Contemptuously, he has tried to take advantage of the Defendant's inexperience in legal matters. The Accuser must be imprisoned for his perjury alone.

"Your Eminence, I request that the Accuser be referred to the Disciplinary Tribunal. I submit that the punishment be to the maximum in severity, to render him totally ineffective, not only in the life of this Defendant, but also in the multitude of lives he aims to destroy."

The woman's Advocate would never be an object of complacency. Every person had an opinion about him. Neutrality was impossible. She knew his tenderness and compassion and had just seen his grand authority to uphold goodness. For her, he was excellence personified. Those who chose to reject and treat him with dishonor were foolish indeed.

It was time for the Judge to bring the case to its conclusion.

The Judge spoke: "In summing up this case, the charges made by the Accuser against the Defendant appear to belong to someone else. In the records of this court, there is only one documented example in which the full weight of humanity's crimes was borne by an innocent man. He took them as his own and transferred his status of innocence to those who desired it. No evidence against the Defendant in this court exists. I rule that the Accuser's evidence is inadmissible. Defendant, through your Advocate's defense, you have your liberty." The woman's heart began to sing instead of cry. The Judge had been shrewd and perceptive. His words were concise, and he had reached his conclusion without doubt or confusion. He knew the law—almost as if he had written it himself.

The Judge continued: "In this courtroom of heaven, I bring to the attention of everyone that change of heart in any criminal toward social harmony does not come through punishment. It comes by belief in the values of goodness. Whether there are ten laws or two laws, love cannot be dictated or enforced. This Defendant shows the voluntary regard for the quality of the life of others, which is the universal solution to society's problems."

At one time, the woman had thought that judges only wanted to punish crime because of the deterrent effect such punishment would have. But now she saw that this Judge obviously took no pleasure in observing evil and doling out its consequences. He had shown her boundless mercy, and she confidently received it. As the Judge spoke, a composite image flashed across her mind. She saw the figure of her Advocate superimposed upon the figure of the Judge. As she looked again at the Judge, he appeared in the same way that her Advocate had done a few moments ago.

The Judge then addressed the Accuser: "You, the Accuser, I find 'Guilty.' I need no more evidence to make this verdict. All costs are awarded to the Defendant. I order full restitution of property stolen from this Defendant, as well as compensation of one-hundred-fold magnitude for pain and suffering. I sentence you, the Accuser, to imprisonment for the term of your life, in order to protect others from your schemes."

For a moment, the woman considered the Judge's tone of voice. How could he show profound mercy to her, but yet mete out severe punishment to the Accuser (vile as he was)? The two were opposing reactions from the same source. She reminded herself that when purity was mixed with a foreign substance, it became impurity. The Judge had to maintain the standard of goodness, or corruption would destroy humanity.

The Accuser's face contorted with extreme, murderous hatred toward the Judge and her Advocate. To the woman's amazement, her fear of this hideous person had dissipated. Then she understood why. She had integrated the legal protection of her Advocate deep into her being. The Accuser was removed from the courtroom, his eyes twitching with new counter-plans of attack.

As the hearing ended, the woman remembered her before-life and felt fear: the fear of having been caught just in time—a fraction of a moment before disaster. This experience in the courtroom of heaven was undeniable. Truth hit with authenticity and did not have to be scientifically verified.

"Hell! That was my destination! How close I came!

That's what frightens me."

Finally, in the chambers of court, the woman spoke to her Advocate. "You have accomplished a fundamental change in me. Everyone who knew me can see the result. I trust you as a child trusts a loving father. In that dream-like experience, I saw you take the fury of punishment that my crimes deserved. I was not living the ways set out in your book. Yet you allowed your impeccable reputation to be trampled like rubbish. When you died a criminal's death on my account, I witnessed it through the eyes of my mind. Thank you for showing me how to conquer the evil power within my nature, as well as its controller."

As the woman watched her Advocate's face, she saw a mixture of peace, pleasure in her gratitude and grief. No doubt he had rescued, defended and restored many like her. Yet she sensed that many had walked away from him as if he meant nothing to them. She wondered how those who saw his sacrifice, as she had done, could have turned away. It was costly to love and care, and it seemed he loved and cared for everyone—even those who had given up on themselves.

The woman spoke to her Advocate again: "My life is transformed. My broken heart is mended. My captivity is ended. All that was stolen has been returned. Your character cannot be tarnished no matter what slander or persecution comes. In loving you, I will love others, and tell them about you. Love never fails."

Her Advocate replied in measured words: "A fearful day of divine import will come with vengeance on evil, wrought on mass scale. There are many that have become spiritually apathetic, have followed false doctrine, led others into immorality and error, and pretended to be holy. Many do not even recognize the wretchedness of their hearts. They have been blinded spiritually. Encourage others to accept the opportunity for reconciliation with God."

When the woman heard these words, she perceived the dread of that day. He was warning her so that she, in turn, would warn others. In that way, many would have the opportunity to be rescued before it was too late. She knew that she had reached a point of departure, and she entered her earth-life again.

The experience in the courtroom of heaven was over. However, the spirit of truth, like blue-red light, warmed her chest cavity, and love surged within her heart. A rushing sound bombarded her ears so that she spoke lyrical, unique words. No longer could she keep silent, although her account was foreign to many. Those who had desired and sought truth heard, and wonderful events ensued. Yet she still needed to make sense of this experience. Probably, in her subconscious state, God had compressed the years of her meditations, and had carried her through the process of releasing her past. Mentally, she had converted these thoughts and experiences into a personal drama, and yet she didn't claim to have had a vision from God. Above all else, she knew she had glimpsed God's glory.

The period prior to her appointment in the courtroom of heaven, she renamed "the former things." The events from this time seemed so far removed from her new life that it was as if they were a bag of old clothes to be thrown out. Happily, the woman recalled her Advocate's advice: "Make a radical change in your life, for the rule of heaven is what is real, and your future is filled with hope."

Miraculously, even in her earth-life, that unique membrane stayed intact. When corruption targeted her, it disintegrated upon contact. She continued to receive her Advocate's comfort, guidance and strength. Her greatest knowledge of him was that of intimacy: a place without barriers.

Finally, he who is Truth said: "Do not be afraid. I am the first and the last. I am with you always."

How limited is man to know the mysteries of the universe created by One who makes everything beautiful in its time.

SCRIPTURES FOR APPLICATION TO YOUR LIFE

The following topic headings are relative to this book only, and they are not intended to be comprehensive in meaning.

God's Timing
There is a time for everything, and a season for every activity under heaven (Ecclesiastes 3:1).

Now Choose Life
This day I call heaven and earth as witnesses against you that I have set before you life and death, blessings and curses. Now choose life, so that you and your children may live (Deuteronomy 30:19).

Ridiculed About Performing a Miracle
They laughed at him, knowing that she was dead. But he took her by the hand and said, "My child, get up!" Her spirit returned, and at once she stood up. Then Jesus told them to give her something to eat (Luke 8:53-55).

What Is Done in Secret Will Be Known
For there is nothing hidden that will not be disclosed, and nothing concealed that will not be known or brought out into the open (Luke 8:17).

A Sustained Search Gets an Answer

Ask and it will be given to you; seek and you will find; knock and the door will be opened to you. For everyone who asks receives; he who seeks finds; and to him who knocks, the door will be opened (Matthew 7:7-8).

The Evil One Denies God's Sovereignty

Who is the liar? It is the man who denies that Jesus is the Christ. Such a man is the antichrist—he denies the Father and the Son (1 John 2:22).

The Reason Society Lacks Peace

You have heard that it was said, "Love your neighbor and hate your enemy." But I tell you: Love your enemies and pray for those who persecute you, that you may be sons of your Father in heaven (Matthew 5:43-45).

No One Is Without Sin

Who can say, "I have kept my heart pure; I am clean and without sin"? (Proverbs 20:9)

Nothing Is Worth the Loss of Eternal Life

What good is it for a man to gain the whole world, yet forfeit his soul? Or what can a man give in exchange for his soul? If anyone is ashamed of me and my words in this adulterous and sinful generation, the Son of Man will be ashamed of him when he comes in his Father's glory with the holy angels. And he said to them, "I tell you the truth, some who are standing

here will not taste death before they see the kingdom of God come with power" (Mark 8:36–9:1).

Do Not Find Fault With God in How He Made You

Woe to him who quarrels with his Maker, to him who is but a potsherd among the potsherds on the ground. Does the clay say to the potter, "What are you making?" Does your work say, "He has no hands"? (Isaiah 45:9)

But who are you, O man, to talk back to God? Shall what is formed say to him who formed it, "Why did you make me like this?" (Romans 9:20)

What You Think Equals the Actual Behavior Spiritually

You have heard that it was said to the people long ago, "Do not murder, and anyone who murders will be subject to judgment." But I tell you that anyone who is angry with his brother will be subject to judgment. Again, anyone who says to his brother, "Raca," is answerable to the Sanhedrin. But anyone who says, "You fool!" will be in danger of the fire of hell.... But I tell you that anyone who looks at a woman lustfully has already committed adultery with her in his heart (Matthew 5:21–28).

All Must Plead Guilty Before God

For all have sinned and fall short of the glory of God (Romans 3:23).

The Real Enemy Is Invisible

For our struggle is not against flesh and blood, but against the rulers, against the authorities, against the powers of this dark world and against the spiritual forces of evil in the heavenly realms (Ephesians 6:12).

We Have Spiritual Armor to Stand Firm

Therefore put on the full armor of God, so that when the day of evil comes, you may be able to stand your ground, and after you have done everything, to stand. Stand firm then, with the belt of truth buckled around your waist, with the breastplate of righteousness in place, and with your feet fitted with the readiness that comes from the gospel of peace. In addition to all this, take up the shield of faith, with which you can extinguish all the flaming arrows of the evil one. Take the helmet of salvation and the sword of the Spirit, which is the word of God (Ephesians 6:13-17).

God Gave His Son to Rescue Us

For God did not send his Son into the world to condemn the world, but to save the world through him (John 3:17).

Jesus Chose Us So That We Might Bear Fruit

You did not choose me, but I chose you and appointed you to go and bear fruit—fruit that will last. Then the Father will give you whatever you ask in my name (John 15:16)

Jesus Christ Didn't Come to Judge Us

For God did not send his Son into the world to condemn the world, but to save the world through him (John 3:17).

Satan Is a Murderer and a Liar

You belong to your father, the devil, and you want to carry out your father's desire. He was a murderer from the beginning, not holding to the truth, for there is no truth in him. When he lies, he speaks his native language, for he is a liar and the father of lies (John 8:44).

Human Nature Has Defiantly Wanted to Take the One Thing Denied Them

And the LORD God commanded the man, "You are free to eat from any tree in the garden; but you must not eat from the tree of the knowledge of good and evil, for when you eat of it you will surely die."

...Now the serpent was more crafty than any of the wild animals the LORD God had made. He said to the woman, "Did God really say, 'You must not eat from any tree in the garden'?"

The woman said to the serpent, "We may eat fruit from the trees in the garden, but God did say, 'You must not eat fruit from the tree that is in the middle of the garden, and you must not touch it, or you will die.'"

"You will not surely die," the serpent said to the woman. "For God knows that when you eat of it your eyes will be opened, and you will be like God, knowing good and evil."

When the woman saw that the fruit of the tree was good for food and pleasing to the eye, and also desirable for gaining wisdom, she took some and ate it. She also gave some to her husband, who was with her, and he ate it (Genesis 2:16–3:6).

Jesus Christ's Divine Commission
The Spirit of the Lord is on me, because he has anointed me to preach good news to the poor. He has sent me to proclaim freedom for the prisoners and recovery of sight for the blind, to release the oppressed, to proclaim the year of the Lord's favor (Luke 4:18).

Dig Deep into God's Word to Prepare for Trials
He is like a man building a house, who dug down deep and laid the foundation on rock. When a flood came, the torrent struck that house but could not shake it, because it was well built (Luke 6:48).

The Lord Desires What Is Hidden to Be Seen
For whatever is hidden is meant to be disclosed, and whatever is concealed is meant to be brought out into the open (Mark 4:22).

Choose Life and Blessing
This day I call heaven and earth as witnesses against you that I have set before you life and death, blessings and curses. Now choose life, so that you and your children may live and that you may love the LORD your God, listen to his voice, and hold fast to him. For the LORD is your life, and he will give you many years in the land he swore to give to your fathers, Abraham, Isaac and Jacob (Deuteronomy 30:19-20).

Only through Jesus Christ Can Man's
Inherited Sinful Nature Be Made Righteous
Who can bring what is pure from the impure? No one!
(Job 14:4)

The Lord's Compassion
When Jesus saw the crowds, he had compassion on them, because they were harassed and helpless, like sheep without a shepherd (Matthew 9:36).

The Goodness of God Leads Man to Repentance
Do you show contempt for the riches of his kindness, tolerance and patience, not realizing that God's kindness leads you toward repentance? (Romans 2:4)

Jesus Christ Opens the Door of
Opportunity for Kingdom Purposes
To the angel of the church in Philadelphia write: These are the words of him who is holy and true, who holds the key of David. What he opens no one can shut, and what he shuts no one can open (Revelation 3:7).

Jesus Christ Freed Us From the Fear of Death
Since the children have flesh and blood, he too shared in their humanity so that by his death he might destroy him who holds the power of death—that is, the devil— and free those who all their lives were held in slavery by their fear of death (Hebrews 2:14-15).

God's Peace in the Midst of a Crisis
And the peace of God, which transcends all understanding, will guard your hearts and your minds in Christ Jesus (Philippians 4:7).

The God of the Universe Cares for Man
What is man that you are mindful of him, the son of man that you care for him? (Psalm 8:4)

Celebrate the Splendor of all God Has Created
He has made everything beautiful in its time. He has also set eternity in the hearts of men; yet they cannot fathom what God has done from beginning to end. I know that there is nothing better for men than to be happy and do good while they live. That everyone may eat and drink, and find satisfaction in all his toil—this is the gift of God.

I know that everything God does will endure forever; nothing can be added to it and nothing taken from it. God does it so that men will revere him (Ecclesiastes 3:11-14).

To Commit One Offense Against God Is to Contravene His Will and His Whole Law
If you really keep the royal law found in Scripture, "Love your neighbor as yourself," you are doing right. But if you show favoritism, you sin and are convicted by the law as lawbreakers. For whoever keeps the whole law and yet stumbles at just one point is guilty of breaking all of it (James 2:8-10).

There Is No Need to Fear
When the Lord Fights for You

Do not be afraid of them; the LORD your God himself will fight for you (Deuteronomy 3:22).

Take Ownership of God's Promises

See, the LORD your God has given you the land. Go up and take possession of it as the LORD, the God of your fathers, told you. Do not be afraid; do not be discouraged (Deuteronomy 1:21).

Knowing the Truth Sets Us Free

Then you will know the truth, and the truth will set you free (John 8:32).

Pilate Could Not Find Jesus Guilty

"What is truth?" Pilate asked. With this he went out again to the Jews and said, "I find no basis for a charge against him" (John 18:38).

Innocence Has Been Put on Trial Before

"If I said something wrong," Jesus replied, "testify as to what is wrong. But if I spoke the truth, why did you strike me?" (John 18:23)

Satan Accused God That Job Loved God Only
Because of Blessings

"Does Job fear God for nothing?" Satan replied. "Have you not put a hedge around him and his household and everything he has? You have blessed the work of his hands, so that his flocks and herds are spread throughout the land. But stretch out your hand and strike everything he has, and he will surely curse you to your face" (Job 1:9-11).

We Now Can Live According to the Spirit

Therefore, there is now no condemnation for those who are in Christ Jesus, because through Christ Jesus the law of the Spirit of life set me free from the law of sin and death. For what the law was powerless to do in that it was weakened by the sinful nature, God did by sending his own Son in the likeness of sinful man to be a sin offering. And so he condemned sin in sinful man, in order that the righteous requirements of the law might be fully met in us, who do not live according to the sinful nature but according to the Spirit (Romans 8:1-4).

Happy Are Those Who Hear and Obey God

Blessed rather are those who hear the word of God and obey it (Luke 11:28).

Satanic Pride

I will ascend above the tops of the clouds; I will make myself like the most High (Isaiah 14:14).

When You Are Born Again, Your Past Is Dead

Therefore, if anyone is in Christ, he is a new creation; the old has gone, the new has come! (2 Cor. 5:17)

All Have Sinned Against God

All have sinned and fall short of the glory of God (Romans 3:23).

The Lord Takes Hold of Your Hand and Helps You

For I am the LORD, your God, who takes hold of your right hand and says to you, Do not fear; I will help you (Isaiah 41:13).

The Lord Will Never Leave You Nor Forsake You

Be strong and courageous. Do not be afraid or terrified because of them, for the LORD your God goes with you; he will never leave you nor forsake you (Deuteronomy 31:6).

Do Not Be Discouraged, For God Is With You to the End

David also said to Solomon his son, "Be strong and courageous, and do the work. Do not be afraid or discouraged, for the LORD God, my God, is with you. He will not fail you or forsake you until all the work for the service of the temple of the LORD is finished" (1 Chronicles 28:20).

Stand Firm and See How the Lord Delivers You

You will not have to fight this battle. Take up your positions; stand firm and see the deliverance the LORD will give you, O Judah and Jerusalem. Do not be afraid; do not be discouraged. Go out to face them tomorrow, and the LORD will be with you (2 Chronicles 20:17).

Jesus Christ Chose Each of Us Before We Chose Him, That We Should Bear Fruit

You did not choose me, but I chose you and appointed you to go and bear fruit—fruit that will last. Then the Father will give you whatever you ask in my name (John 15:16).

Contempt for God Will Not Go Unpunished

He who mocks the poor shows contempt for their Maker; whoever gloats over disaster will not go unpunished (Proverbs 17:5).

The Divine Exchange

God made him who had no sin to be sin for us, so that in him we might become the righteousness of God (2 Corinthians 5:21).

The Two Commandments

"The most important one," answered Jesus, "is this: 'Hear, O Israel, the Lord our God, the Lord is one. Love the Lord your God with all your heart and with all your soul and with all your mind and with all your strength.' The second is this: 'Love your neighbor as yourself.' There is no commandment greater than these" (Mark 12:29-31).

Love Never Fails

Love never fails. But where there are prophecies, they will cease; where there are tongues, they will be stilled; where there is knowledge, it will pass away (1 Corinthians 13:8).

Jesus Christ Commends, Censures and Warns His Church

"To the angel of the church in Ephesus write:

These are the words of him who holds the seven stars in his right hand and walks among the seven golden lampstands: I know your deeds, your hard work and your perseverance. I know that you cannot tolerate wicked men, that you have tested those who claim to be apostles but are not, and have found them false. You have persevered and have endured hardships for my name, and have not grown weary.

Yet I hold this against you: You have forsaken your first love. Remember the height from which you have fallen! Repent and do the things you did at first. If you do not repent, I will come to you and remove your lampstand from its place. But you have this in your favor: You hate the practices of the Nicolaitans, which I also hate.

He who has an ear, let him hear what the Spirit says to the churches. To him who overcomes, I will give the right to eat from the tree of life, which is in the paradise of God.

"To the angel of the church in Smyrna write:

These are the words of him who is the First and the Last, who died and came to life again. I know your afflictions and your poverty—yet you are rich! I know the slander of those who say they are Jews and are not, but are a synagogue of Satan. Do not be afraid of what you are about to suffer. I tell you, the devil will put some of you in prison to test you, and you will suffer persecution for ten days. Be faithful, even to the point of death, and I will give you the crown of life.

He who has an ear, let him hear what the Spirit says to the churches. He who overcomes will not be hurt at all by the second death.

"To the angel of the church in Pergamum write:

These are the words of him who has the sharp, double-edged sword. I know where you live—where Satan has his throne. Yet you remain true to my name. You did not renounce your faith in me, even in the days of Antipas, my faithful witness, who was put to death in your city—where Satan lives.

Nevertheless, I have a few things against you: You have people there who hold to the teaching of Balaam, who taught Balak to entice the Israelites to sin by eating food sacrificed to idols and by committing sexual immorality. Likewise you also have those who hold to the teaching of the Nicolaitans. Repent therefore! Otherwise, I will soon come to you and will fight against them with the sword of my mouth.

He who has an ear, let him hear what the Spirit says to the churches. To him who overcomes, I will give some of the hidden manna. I will also give him a white stone with a new name written on it, known only to him who receives it.

"To the angel of the church in Thyatira write:

These are the words of the Son of God, whose eyes are like blazing fire and whose feet are like burnished bronze. I know your deeds, your love and faith, your service and perseverance, and that you are now doing more than you did at first.

Nevertheless, I have this against you: You tolerate that woman Jezebel, who calls herself a prophetess. By her teaching she misleads my servants into sexual immorality and the eating of food sacrificed to idols. I have given her time to repent of her immorality, but she is unwilling. So I will cast her on a bed of suffering, and I will make those who commit adultery with her suffer intensely, unless they repent of her ways. I will strike her children dead. Then all the churches will know that I am he who searches hearts and minds, and I will repay each of you according to your deeds. Now I say to the rest of you in Thyatira, to you who do not hold to her teaching and have not learned Satan's so-called deep secrets (I will not impose any other burden on you): Only hold on to what you have until I come.

To him who overcomes and does my will to the end, I will give authority over the nations— He will rule them with an iron scepter; he will dash them to pieces like pottery'—just as I have received authority from my Father. I will also give him the morning star. He who has an ear, let him hear what the Spirit says to the churches.

"To the angel of the church in Sardis write:

These are the words of him who holds the seven spirits of God and the seven stars. I know your deeds; you have a reputation of being alive, but you are dead. Wake up! Strengthen what remains and is about to die, for I have not found your deeds complete in the sight of my God. Remember, therefore, what you have received and heard; obey it, and repent. But if you do not wake up, I will come like a thief, and you will not know at what time I will come to you.

Yet you have a few people in Sardis who have not soiled their clothes. They will walk with me, dressed in white, for they are worthy. He who overcomes will, like them, be dressed in white. I will never blot out his name from the book of life, but will acknowledge his name before my Father and his angels. He who has an ear, let him hear what the Spirit says to the churches.

"To the angel of the church in Philadelphia write:

These are the words of him who is holy and true, who holds the key of David. What he opens no one can shut, and what he shuts no one can open. I know your deeds. See, I have placed before you an open door that no one can shut. I know that you have little strength, yet you have kept my word and have not denied my name. I will make those who are of the synagogue of Satan, who claim to be Jews though they are not, but are liars—I will make them come and fall down at your feet and acknowledge that I have loved you. Since you have kept my command to endure patiently, I will also keep you from the hour of trial that is going to come upon the whole world to test those who live on the earth.

I am coming soon. Hold on to what you have, so that no one will take your crown. Him who overcomes I will make a pillar in the temple of my God. Never again will he leave it. I will write on him the name of my God and the name of the city of my God, the new Jerusalem, which is coming down out of heaven from my God; and I will also write on him my new name. He who has an ear, let him hear what the Spirit says to the churches.

"To the angel of the church in Laodicea write:

These are the words of the Amen, the faithful and true witness, the ruler of God's creation. I know your deeds, that you are neither cold nor hot. I wish you were either one or the other! So, because you are lukewarm—neither hot nor cold—I am about to spit you out of my mouth. You say, 'I am rich; I have acquired wealth and do not need a thing.' But you do not realize that you are wretched, pitiful, poor, blind and naked" (Revelation 2:1–3:17).

The Gospel Is Good News for Those Who Listen and Respond to the Lord

Repent, for the kingdom of heaven is near (Matthew 3:2).

Jesus Christ Is Eternal

When I saw him, I fell at his feet as though dead. Then he placed his right hand on me and said: "Do not be afraid. I am the First and the Last" (Revelation 1:17).

Jesus Christ Is God With Us—A Great Reassurance

…And surely I am with you always, to the very end of the age (Matthew 28:20).

The Greatness of God Is Immeasurable, Glorious and Beyond Comprehension

He has made everything beautiful in its time. He has also set eternity in the hearts of men; yet they cannot fathom what God has done from beginning to end (Ecclesiastes 3:11).

Dear Reader,

Many will be able to pray the following prayer. However, for some, the struggle is still fierce. Therefore, those people should pray "as if" it is so, because that is the reality of redemption. As noted in the Introduction, the Christian life involves becoming who one already is in Christ. All that is required is to appropriate the promises of God. Let's pray!

Dear Lord God Almighty,
Thank You!
That the essence of my being validates the truth that You are the light of the world.

Thank You!
That the darkness is banished from my life.

Thank You!
That Your still, small voice has quieted my once stormy mind.

Thank You!
That beautiful feelings are now mine: Gone is the ash-heap of my clashing emotions.

Thank You!
That I now have new opportunities, instead of times of chaos and destruction.

I now know who You are, even if in the tiniest way. Yet how can I, a speck on the horizon, ever comprehend the bounty of Your grace, love, mercy and kindness? You are the Maker of all things, and all things exist because of You. Yet You are my Rescuer and the Lover of my soul. How amazing!

Until we meet face to face, lead me by Your Spirit into the place of divine embrace—to live the experience of being one with Christ. It is here that Your Word comes alive, and I become the epistle You created me to be, the vessel to carry Your love letter to others.

My prayer is one of surrender—not of defeat, but of triumph. Thank You for giving me the courage to turn away from everything that displeases You. I give You my life, to live according to Your will, knowing You are the supremely trustworthy One.

Thank You, gracious Lord Jesus!

Amen.

ABOUT THE AUTHOR

Leigh Allison has attained three tertiary qualifications: a General Nursing Certificate, a Bachelor of Arts Degree, and a Certificate in Christian Studies. She has also worked in the Queensland Police Force as a Policewoman Constable, and was later employed by the Australian Public Service.

During the period corresponding to her working life, she suffered a biochemical form of mental illness that began in early adulthood. Leigh Allison experienced the other end of the spectrum, watching her self-image disintegrate into hopelessness and disgrace during the episodes of her illness. Wrong diagnoses, ECT, becoming a regulated patient and two attempts at suicide, brought home to her the realization that only Jesus Christ could save her physically, as well as spiritually. Through a relationship with Him, Leigh Allison found salvation, healing, restoration and peace far beyond her expectations and hope.

To contact the author for speaking engagements
or
if you would like the free article entitled,

Some Things That Helped Me

please e-mail Leigh Allison:
lallison57@gmail.com